FRAMES AND FORKS

FRAMES AND FORKS

Roy Bacon

OSPREY

Published in 1989 by Osprey Publishing
59 Grosvenor Street, London W1X 9DA

British Library Cataloguing in
Publication Data

Bacon, Roy H. (Roy Hunt)
    Frames and forks.
    1. Motorcycles. Restoration
    I. Title   II. Series
    629.28'775

ISBN 0-85045-861-7

Editor Ian Penberthy
Design Martin Richards

Filmset and printed by
BAS Printers Limited
Over Wallop, Hampshire, Great Britain

PAGE 1 **Hesketh frame with headstock and rear fork bearings joined by fairly straight tubes**

COVER/PAGE 3 **The Norton Featherbed frame set the standard for many years and combined with their Roadholder telescopic forks to give hairline steering to Manx, Inter and ohv singles, as well as the twin seen here**

Contents

Acknowledgements

The sixth in this series of books for motorcycle restorers deals with the frame and forks, so it includes the suspension system. These parts may lack the glamour of the engine, but they are the skeleton that the rest of the machine relies on for support and, thus, are as vital.

As with previous books, I have to thank Ken Hallworth, of *Old Bike Mart*, for his help in reading the manuscript, reminding me of things I had missed and pointing out errors. All writers benefit from having their work reviewed and edited, and I am fortunate that Ken agreed to undertake this task for me.

The photographs for this book came from the EMAP archives, which hold the old *Motor Cycle Weekly* files, *Motor Cycle News*, courtesy of editor Malcolm Gough, and my own files. Many were taken specifically to illustrate this book. Some of the photographs came from commercial sources, and in this respect I have to thank BMW, Gilera, Girling, Harley-Davidson, Hesketh, Honda, Hossack, Lambretta, Moto Guzzi, Puch, Samefa, Suzuki and Vespa. Friends whose photographs I used were Don Morley, Malcolm Newell and Donald Page.

A number of line drawings were used where these showed details better than a photograph. Most were from contemporary magazines or manufacturers' manuals, and I trust they will serve to amplify the text. All borrowed items were returned to their files after publication, and I have tried to make contact to clear copyright. If my letter failed to reach you, or I have used an unmarked print without realizing this, please accept my apologies.

Finally my thanks to the staff at Osprey who, as always, helped to bring this book to its final form.

Roy Bacon
Niton, Isle of Wight January 1989

ACKNOWLEDGEMENTS

Exotic custom job based on Yamaha engine unit, monoshock rear and leading-link forks in bottom-link style

Introduction

A motorcycle's frame and forks provide the skeleton to which the rest of the machine is attached, even though that rest may be an integral part of the structure. They work together with the wheels, the machine's weight and the rider to offer both good roadholding and precise steering at best, or weaves, wobbles and worry at worst.

This book deals with the restoration of the parts rather than the theory behind their design, their relation and reaction to each other, and the way they combine to give the required effect. These are subjective matters, as much determined by the rider's style and demands on the chassis as the technology involved.

For more on the theory and how that is turned into practice in design and manufacture, you are directed to *Motorcycle Chassis Design* by Foale and Willoughby, published by Osprey, which is now the standard reference work on the subject. This volume is more concerned with dealing with what you have, although alterations are not ignored.

An endeavour has been made to at least mention all the various forms of frames, forks and rear suspensions that have appeared since the dawn of motorcycling. It is, perhaps, inevitable that something will have been missed along the way, as chassis design has followed some obscure paths at times, but all the major forms are included.

The aim of this book is to assist and guide the reader in the restoration of the frame and forks of his or her motorcycle. It is hoped that the result will be safe and sound in all respects, and every endeavour has been made to offer helpful and sound advice. However, the frame and forks are only part of the complete motorcycle chassis, and the effects of the other components must not be forgotten. In addition, the outcome, when in use, is highly subjective, and for those reasons the onus is always with the reader to ensure that all work is carried out in a sensible manner, having due regard for safety precautions.

Neither the author nor publisher can accept any liability for anything contained in this book, which may result in loss, damage or injury, and the book is only available for purchase or loan on that basis.

In particular, the reader is reminded that suspension springs are often held in place under heavy loads and, therefore, must be released with care. Thus, if you ignore the oft-quoted warning about using the correct tools when dealing with a Triumph sprung hub and a spring goes through the ceiling, via your person, it is your fault and nothing to do with me or us!

Equally unconventional Ariel Leader with pressed-steel, box-section frame and trailing-link forks

CHAPTER 1
Design and types

The motorcycle evolved from the bicycle by the simple expedient of bolting on an engine, at some point, and linking this to a wheel with a belt. It was preceded by the tricycle, which carried the engine near the rear axle but, again, this began with a cycle frame.

The tricycle soon faded from popularity, except in the three-wheeler car form, but the motorcycle went from strength to strength. It was soon realized that the extra weight, speed and vibration was too much for the stock bicycle parts, so these were strengthened as required, although this took some while.

The mainstream motorcycle continued with its cycle-type construction of the frame, using lugs and tubes, for many years, but alongside it there developed other methods employing the same or alternative materials. Some of these thought to be modern methods, may have been tried many years earlier, and may have been successful or abandoned due to technical problems or customer resistance.

While most frames are constructed from tubing, there are many examples which use pressings that are welded or bolted together. These may take the conventional form to surround and support the engine and gearbox, or may be of the spine type with the engine unit suspended from the frame. Less common is the use of alloy castings in the frame structure, but these are to be found and, in one case, comprise the complete frame. Composite methods of

LEFT **Scott twin with early form of telescopic forks, despite the girder appearance** construction are not uncommon, both tube and sheet being employed and in many different arrangements.

The tyres and saddle provided the suspension system to begin with, but this was soon improved on by allowing the front wheel a small degree of movement. This continued to remain restrained for many years, due to the form of suspension linkage used in most cases, and it was not until well into the post-war era that much increase was generally adopted. Later still came long fork travel for off-road machines.

At the front, the first machines used the bicycle fork, which was rapidly strengthened, and then various forms of link girders. These came in a variety of designs and offered enough movement, strength and an easy correction for sidecar use. In the post-war years, the telescopic fork gradually took over, but was no novelty, for it had been seen in one form on the Scott, around 1908, and on BMW and Nimbus models by 1935.

The most common post-war alternative to the telescopic fork was the leading-link type, which included the Earles. The latter was characterized by long fork arms linked by a cross-member behind the wheel, whereas the normal leading-links were short and only connected by the wheel spindle. The design dated from the earliest days, as did the trailing-link type, which was never so popular due to the problems of providing neatly mounted pivot points.

In addition to these main forms of suspension, there is also the hub-centre type. This has existed for many years, the Ner-a-Car being an early example, and is effectively a leading-link form with the link pivoted from the machine and the wheel turning on a kingpin at the front end of the link. It is always difficult to arrange for the link to clear the tyre on full lock, and a variation, the Hossack, has the kingpin pivot above the wheel. This is held between blades, which are located by wishbones to the frame with ball-joints at the front for the blade assembly to turn in. The design is, in effect, the same as one half of a car's independent front suspension, with the wheel held in an extension of the kingpin.

At the rear very few machines had any suspension, other than that provided by the tyre and saddle, until the post-war era. Even then, it was by no means universal for many years, while it was some time before the pivoted fork took over completely. Examples of all can be found on Edwardian models so, once more, there is seldom anything new.

Wartime Harley-Davidson with bottom-link forks and plunger rear suspension among its features

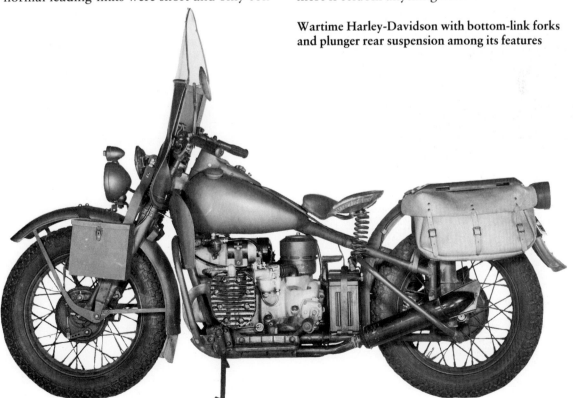

It is essential that the action of the suspension system is considered apart from its control medium when reviewing the alternative designs. With a couple of exceptions, rear suspension is by plunger or pivoted fork, and these produce straight and curved wheel-spindle movements respectively. Plunger suspension is normally controlled directly by springs mounted in line with the plunger and wheel movement, but the pivoted-fork type can have far more variation. This ranges from the traditional twin suspension units, usually with springs and hydraulic damping, through all manner of link mechanisms, and on to modern rising-rate designs.

The same rule should be applied to the front suspension, where leading- and trailing-link types often have a complex connection between the link and the suspension medium.

Regardless of what this is, the wheel still moves about an axis.

Design features

The way in which a motorcycle behaves on road or track is basically determined by various measurements and dimensions. It is further refined by a whole host of lesser features, along with their development. Most are set by the design and will not be varied by the owner, but a couple may change to suit the attachment of a sidecar, or several can be altered or set by an owner when building up a special.

One important factor is the wheelbase, which is the distance between the wheel spindles. It will be short for trials models to enable them to manoeuvre in tight situations, and long on tourers for directional stability.

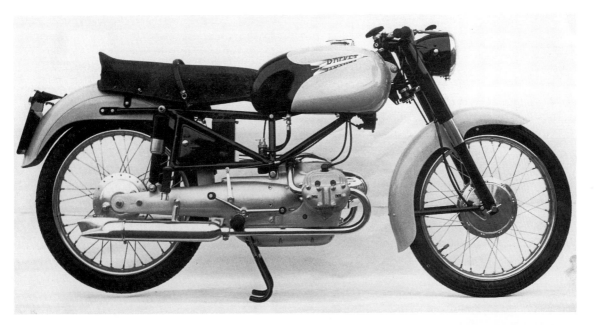

ABOVE **Italian IMN Rocket; the complete engine, gearbox and shaft-drive package pivots from the spine frame**

LEFT **Francis-Barnett Fulmar with tubular spine frame under the bodywork and leading-link front forks**

Road racing calls for something less to maintain high-speed stability while giving the quick handling needed when cornering, and sports models vary between this and the tourer, depending on the market niche they are aimed at.

Except for hub-centre designs, the front forks pivot in the frame headstock, and this is laid back in relation to the ground at what is known as the rake angle. At the bottom of the forks is the wheel spindle, and if a vertical line is drawn from this to the ground, it will fall behind one taken through the headstock to the ground. The distance between the two points is called the trail, and for a solo may lie between 2 and 4 in., but is best reduced for a sidecar to lighten the steering.

The trail may be affected by the position of the various detail parts, their size and the front wheel diameter. Normally, it is the only dimension concerning steering and handling that an owner may alter, and this can be done in a variety of ways. Most come about because the wheel spindle is set ahead of the steering-axis line through the headstock in order to arrive at the required trail. This offset, as it is called, is made up of two components. One is the offset of the yokes or crowns, above and below

the headstock, in front of the steering axis, and the other the offset of the wheel spindle ahead of the fork leg centre-line of telescopics. This second dimension is commonly zero, so the offset is set by the yokes, but where it exists the forks may be referred to as the offset- or forward-spindle type.

It should be noted that while it is normal for the headstock and fork legs of telescopics to lay parallel to each other, it is not always so. Forks do exist where the leg angle differs slightly from that of the headstock to produce particular effects on the steering and handling.

Part of the handling equation comes from the combined weight of rider and machine, plus any passenger, and how this sits relative to the wheels. Other items which all play their parts are frame stiffness, machine speed, tyre size and brake loads.

None of the above is of much concern if you are simply restoring a machine, although it always helps to know the 'why' as well as the 'how' of a particular design. It becomes much more important if you seek to modify any aspects of any part involved or to use different components. Thus, a change of wheel diameter can have some minor effect, while fitting one make of forks to another frame needs to be well thought out. The final step along this road is the special, perhaps with a new frame design, and before any moves are made in this direction, some basic design studies must be carried out.

Do not attempt any change to the machine

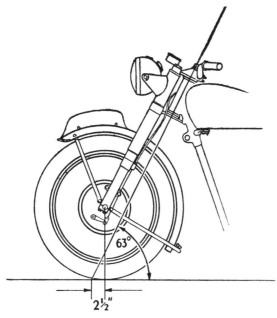

without considering all these aspects, plus others such as ground and cornering clearance, otherwise you may be in trouble. Motorcycle steering and handling is not a simple subject, nor one that all of us are suited to evaluate. Fortunately for restorers, their tasks are the more familiar ones of repair and renovation.

LEFT The basic front end features of head angle, or rake, and the trail, which is reduced for sidecar work

BELOW The innovative Phasar with a Kawasaki Z1300 engine unit in a feet-forward frame with hub-centre steering

CHAPTER 2
Tools and techniques

Frames and forks call for rather different tools than engines or electrics but, as always, you can only attempt what you are equipped for. Perhaps more than in other areas, there are definite stages in what can be attempted that are set by your tools. These are, effectively, simple spanner work, repair of detail fitments by welding, and frame straightening.

It is important to recognize these stages and plan accordingly, either to acquire the equipment and learn how to use it, or to farm out certain aspects of the work. That decision will depend on various factors, but consider what is best in both the long- and short-term before buying any expensive gear.

As always, if you approach the tasks with confidence and think out each stage in advance, the problems may well melt away.

have everything you will need. At the same time, inspect it with a critical eye and discard anything which is not of good quality, for such tools can easily hurt you and damage parts if they slip at the wrong moment.

You will need a selection of hand tools, spanners being of the appropriate sizes to suit the thread system used on the machine. Be wary of some British models of the late 1960s period, which may combine some Unified threads with the older Whitworth form so that you will need both spanner types.

In addition to the more usual spanner sizes, you are likely to need some much larger ones and specials to deal with the front forks. Often, the headrace adjustment and fork top nuts are both large and thin, which may mean a special will be needed or that a socket must be ground

Tools

First, think about what you will be doing and then review your equipment to see whether you

Big nut spanner, as used on Norton Commando forks when adjusting their bearings

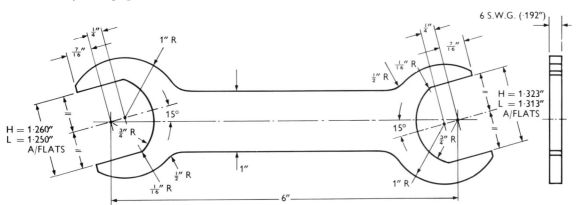

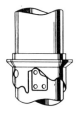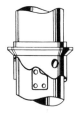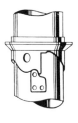

FIRST POSITION LIGHT LOAD **SECOND POSITION MEDIUM LOAD** **THIRD POSITION HEAVY LOAD**

ABOVE Typical suspension unit, where a C-spanner is needed to set the cam ring preload

down to remove its internal chamfer to prevent it slipping. Where the latter applies, it is imperative that the socket is held squarely on the nut or bolt head, otherwise it will slip with consequent damage to the machine's parts and owner's hands.

These areas may call for a hook or C-spanner, and if they do, make quite sure you have one that fits without any danger of it slipping. A hammer and drift are not an effective substitute and should not be used, although you may well find a need to repair the damage caused by such practices in the past.

Hook spanners are just one step away from some of the special tools you may need, especially for working on the fork legs. It is common for there to be a circlip or a threaded ring at the top of the sliding leg to hold everything in place, and removing this can be tricky without the correct tool. In some cases, the ring will be part of a chrome-plated extension sleeve which will lack any means of unscrewing it. Even where a cross-hole is provided, it can easily allow the sleeve to be distorted if the thread is tight, so an alternative may be needed. This can be a leather strap-wrench, which can often be improvised using a length of belt and two ring spanners to lock it into postion with enough grip.

ABOVE RIGHT BSA factory tool for pulling fork leg up into top yoke is nice, but a threaded bar will do the job

RIGHT Special tool for removing the oil seal holder from a BSA fork leg, and which can be fabricated from a piece of tube

The rear suspension area can also cause tool problems, even with a simple plunger system. It may be necessary to use a long rod to compress the springs before removal and for assembly, although often this can be done by hand. In some cases, it would be very dangerous to attempt this work without the right tools, so find out before you undo anything.

Rear fork pivots can make trouble, too, especially where the spindle is a press-fit in the frame. In this case, you will need a press to get it out, while if it has seized or is worn, renovation will be even more of a problem. Where a press is needed, it may have to be of quite a size, as it may need to span the frame, provide enough movement to push the pin right out, and accommodate the frame itself, which may be rather unwieldly.

The next stage of equipment is the possession of oxy-acetylene welding gear, as this will allow many frame repairs to be carried out. It can also be used for brazing, heating and metal cutting, so is versatile and really an essential tool for any serious work.

Alloy parts are best welded using the tungsten inert gas (TIG) or metal inert gas (MIG) processes, which can also be used for stainless steel. Avoid arc welding, which carries a risk of electrocution, and take all necessary safety precautions. It can be well worth attending a course at your local technical college to learn how to weld properly, which is best done before buying any equipment.

Working on the frame can mean checking and correcting its alignment. Neither is an easy task, and it may well be best to farm out both

ABOVE **Norton rear plunger unit, as used by racing model, but without any effective damping**

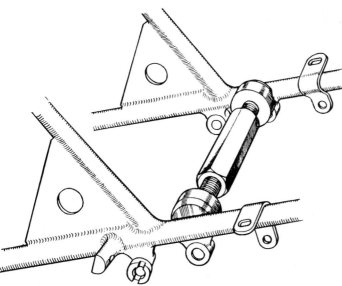

LEFT **Tool for spreading the frame members to allow the rear fork to be removed, as required for some Royal Enfield models**

ABOVE Gilera Saturno with open pivoted-fork frame holding nice engine and gearbox unit

TOP The Foale Project QL machine with BMW power unit and elegant front suspension system

ABOVE RIGHT Pro-link rear suspension on the works Honda of 1980 with links and rising rate

to someone with the necessary equipment and expertise. Alignment checks usually call for a large surface table and a variety of measuring equipment, while repairs often need a brazing hearth and a means of holding the frame by its headstock. The hearth provides more widespread heat than a welding torch, which is less successful where several frame members need to be heated at the same time.

Before you begin any work, do check to see if you will need special tools and make sure you have them before starting. Remember the restorer's adage that the cost of the damage will always be higher than that of the tool you should have used.

Data

Collect the data and any parts lists needed for the work. You will find much that you require in either the machine's handbook or a workshop manual, and with this information can more easily check whether parts or assemblies are still fit for further use. In many cases, the data will mainly concern the headraces, fork springs, damping oil and rear unit details, but more will be needed if the frame has been damaged. To deal with this, you may need dimensional data, which is more likely to be available

for 1960 and later machines than older ones. In part, this is due to the earlier practice of using built-up frames, often with the engine as an essential member, with two or more assemblies bolted together. This made overall checking dimensions less useful and, thus, not always provided.

The parts list will help to determine which parts bolt to the frame and, hence, if there is any damage to correct. Where the machine is complete to begin with, you should have little trouble, but if you are building up from parts, it may not be so easy. The illustrations in the better parts lists often indicate a component's basic shape and how it is attached and relates to its surroundings. The presence, or not, of spacers and washers can also often clarify confusing areas.

It is absolutely vital to make notes of how the parts are positioned before you take anything apart. If this is done diligently, there should be no real trouble on assembly, but if neglected, you will find you just cannot remember the details. It may be the position of the horn, or the order in which stays fit on to a common stud, but forget it you will.

Photographs and notes will keep matters in order and provide a good record. Also, compare what you have with contemporary photographs to determine whether you have inherited changes or not. Be careful in the use of pictures of restored machines if you seek authenticity. If this is the case, the various Osprey marque history and restoration books will assist, as they include photographs from the past.

Coping with large nuts

The tools for these have already been mentioned, but it is worth repeating that they must fit well, otherwise there will be trouble. In addition, it must be remembered that when leaning on the spanner, you must also prevent the rest of the machine moving which can be awkward in some cases.

Otherwise, large nuts should not be a problem, regardless of whether they are undone with a conventional, hook or pin spanner. Left-hand threads are unlikely to be encountered, but do not forget that they exist, since they may well be the cause of a problem.

Nuts and bolts

Reducing the frame to its bare bones will be straightforward if all the screws, nuts and bolts can be released as necessary, but often this is not the case. In far too many cases, it will be because of a butcher having been at work in the past, which inevitably makes the task harder. Much restoration work is simply repairing the bodges of the past caused by some owners not leaving their machines's alone.

Before taking further, more drastic measures, check that the stubborn fastener is not locked by a washer, as sometimes these can be difficult to spot. If you find one, its tab will need to be eased up, and a small chisel is often the best tool to start this job, after which a drift will complete it. Keep all old lock washers, as some may be fit for further use, and all will serve as patterns for replacements.

A second check is for left-hand threads, and in some cases the parts may be marked with an 'L', but not always. The manual may give an answer, as may a careful inspection of any thread that can be seen, although this may not be feasible where parts fit closely together.

The far more common reasons for immovable fixings are rust and corrosion or a thread seizure, which may be due to distortion of the thread form or the part itself. Where the parts have seized, they will not be in very good condition, even when apart, so you can be more brutal than usual when dismantling.

This can mean using a nut-splitter, although it is often impossible to fit one of these bulky tools into place on a motorcycle. The alternative is to cut the nut in half by drilling holes into it before using a chisel to complete the task. Cutting or drilling a bolt head is equally feasible, although sometimes it can be a problem to hold the part still while doing this.

A further solution can be used where a nut and bolt hold a sheet-steel part to a frame lug. If they have seized, or corroded, it can be the very devil to either undo them more than a turn or to cut them away without damaging the parts they hold. With small fastenings, the solution is to slacken them a turn, to make sure they will move, and then simply tighten them until the bolt shears off.

This method also works well when an exposed length of the bolt thread has rusted so that removal of the nut will be a struggle. In other cases, a corroded part may begin to move if it is heated with a welding torch, using a small flame to stop the heat spreading. If a previous owner has used Loctite on the threads, heat will also be needed to destroy the locking bond.

Screws and studs

A screw can be more of a problem than a bolt because the head is often small and easily damaged. In some cases, front fork legs being an example, they may be set in a counterbore and, if this is aluminium, the problem becomes more acute.

The first move with a stubborn screw is to try an impact driver, but always remember the basic rules when using this tool. Firstly, the bit must fit the screw head and have something to work against. Next, it must be held square-on to the screw, and lastly hit it good and hard just once. This may mean arranging a support behind the part to absorb the shock, but it must

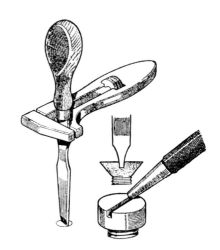

ABOVE **Stubborn screws may need more force, a better blade fit or delicate work with punch and hammer**

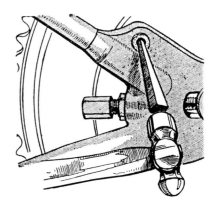

ABOVE **One way of removing broken studs is with a square drift in a drilled hole, but always with care**

be done this way, as a series of light taps will not do the job at all.

If the impact driver has nothing to work on, the answer may be to drill away the screw head. This is easy with crosshead screws, as the driver depression will centre the drill, but it is much more difficult with a slotted head. In addition, removal of the screw head only helps where it holds a part of some depth so that the remaining screw shank can be held and undone.

In most cases, the screw either will hold a piece of sheet in place, or will run into a tapped hole, so it must be removed complete in one piece. This means that the screw will need to have a hole drilled into its centre to allow a stud extractor to be used to remove it. The technique is just the same where a stud is concerned; when these break, it is usally just below the surface of the part.

The essence of the problem is making the hole run down the centre of the screw or stud, which will not be helped by the small size of most that need this attention. It may be feasible to use a drill bush, or some other form of jig, to start the drill in the right place and direction, but it is seldom easy. A little work on the exposed surface with a small rotary cutter may

ABOVE **The Eric Oliver Norton Watsonian outfit with nice straight connections for world championship winning**

BELOW **Classic, welded, duplex cradle frame housing 7R engine and separate gearbox**

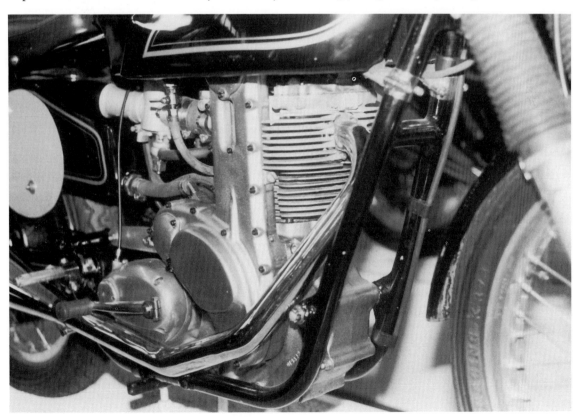

ABOVE **Norman Lido** moped with typical pressed-steel beam frame, but with the front fork links joined by a rear loop

BELOW **BMW** flat-twin with duplex frame, rather forced on it by the engine form and here fitted with plunger rear suspension

make the job easier, but can equally easily cut into the surrounding metal.

Once the initial hole has been produced, it can be enlarged to the necessary size for the stud extractor. This should be screwed into the hole until it locks, after which, continued turning should wind the stud out. It is imperative that this is done with care, as the smaller extractors are quite slender and easily broken

themselves. If this should happen, you really will have a problem, unless you happen to have access to spark-erosion equipment.

An alternative to a stud extractor is the tang of a file, but this, too, can break easily. A further option is to continue drilling and either retap the hole to the original thread, or to repair it with an insert.

Thread inserts

These are a means of reclaiming a damaged or stripped thread, and there are a number of types on the market. One of the best known is the HeliCoil wire-thread insert, made by Armstrong Fastening Systems, as it is very compact and only adds one thread depth to the overall diameter. This is because it is wound from diamond-section wire to form a thread into which the original screw or stud can be fitted, thanks to it having the same number of threads per inch and the correct diameter.

The inserts are easy to fit, but a good job will require some care and the use of the correct tools. The first stage is to drill out the hole to a specified size, which is normally just over the basic thread diameter. Often, the damaged hole will be close to this anyway, which can help. The hole is then tapped using a HeliCoil tap, which is larger than the original thread, but has the same tpi. It must run in square to the surface, otherwise the insert will not be true when installed and the fixing will lean.

A full depth of thread must be cut as, if it is not, the insert will be too tight on the stud. There is a HeliCoil gauge for this, but not all restorers will wish to run to this cost, so an alternative, if the hole is not blind, is to install an insert as a thread check. If tight, the insert can be wound right through, and the hole tapped out further.

When the thread is ready, the metal around the hole should be checked to ensure that it is flat and has not pulled up, while a small countersink may be added to lead the insert in. In normal applications, it is wound in using a HeliCoil tool until it is between a quarter and a half turn below the surface and should then be checked with the stud or screw. The drive tang at the leading end is notched for removal, and HeliCoil offer another tool for this, although most people use the driver of the inserting tool or a small punch of similar size.

A machined insert would do the same job,

The Brough Superior Dream of pre-war days with its leading-link Castle forks

but often there will not be enough room for one, and the same may apply to a double-diameter stud. The HeliCoil, and other similar systems, is very compact and, thus, is often used on any doubtful threads, or even where the fixing has to be removed frequently, as in drain plugs.

Cleaning the parts

This process usually starts when the machine is still in one piece and continues after it has been dismantled. The methods used will depend on the part, its material, its condition

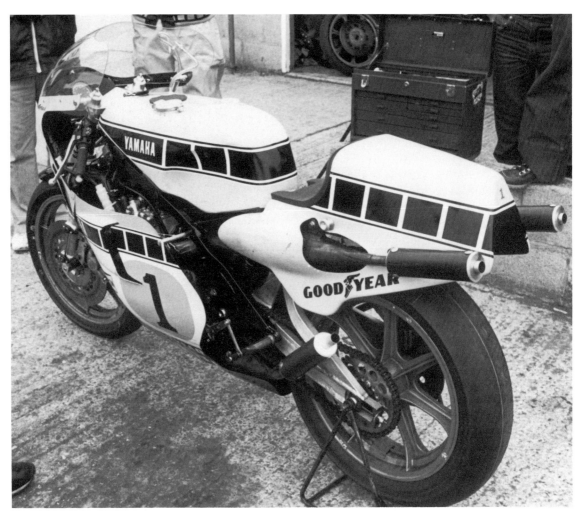

The Kenny Roberts works Yamaha at Silverstone in 1980, with its alloy rear fork controlled by monoshock

and its finish, but most will be painted steel with a few in aluminium. If the parts are in good order, a simple solvent wash will suffice to clean off the dirt and grime, but more often there will be damage, to the part or its finish, or corrosion.

If you intend to keep the original paint, the part will only require cleaning and an inspection of its details but, in most cases, more work will be needed. Paint can be removed by chemical or mechanical means, and the method used will affect the texture of the base metal's surface and the resultant finish.

Alloy parts can be cleaned chemically with household detergent or proprietary cleaners. Most of these are acidic in nature, so the part must be washed thoroughly after cleaning. Household detergent is best used with hot water for the best effect.

Paint can be removed with a chemical stripper, which is quick, efficient and messy. It is also a dangerous substance, so wear full pro-

tective clothing, including gloves and goggles, to avoid contact. Follow the instructions to the letter and check the procedure for dealing with splashes and accidents before you start.

To remove the paint, spread out some newspapers, lay out the parts and paint on the stripper. The paint will soon bubble up and will often lift off in sheets with a little help from a paint scraper. It is imperative that all remnants of the old paint and stripper are removed, after which the parts will need to be cleaned with water or thinners, depending on the stripper base. Dispose of the old paint and paper, which will now be an industrial hazard so is best burnt, although this must be done out of doors and will smell. You may find patches of filler under the paint, and these must also be removed so that you reach bare metal and can fully assess any damage. Do not be tempted to leave the filler in place, as the paint removal will have disturbed it and it could be close to falling away. Like the old paint and stripper, any filler must come off before the new finish is applied or it will lift within a short while.

Mechanical cleaning can be done by scraping the paint away, but is more usually carried out by one of the blasting processes. These vary in severity and will remove both paint and any corrosion caused by the formation of rust. For most cycle parts, aluminous-oxide grit blasting is suitable and not too severe. Avoid iron grit or shot, which can blow holes in sheet steel, while for delicate work consider vapour or bead blasting.

This last is popular, as it leaves a clean, matt surface which is ideal for painting and calls for less masking off than the other, harsher processes. For these, and to protect the fine threads and surfaces when bead blasting, masking is essential. This can be done using tape, nuts, bolts, scrap tube, plate and rubber seals cut from old inner tubes.

All threaded holes and openings leading to the interior of a part need to be blanked off. Thus, a headstock requires a length of studding and end plates, plus a bolt in the grease-nipple hole. Similar techniques will be needed elsewhere to protect close-tolerance holes, and care will be needed at the boundary of the mask to achieve the desired effect. Therefore, that grease-nipple hole should be blocked with a bolt screwed in to the end of its thread, as a screw taken right down to its head would leave a small masked circle. These details mark the concours winner.

Paint and rust can be removed using emery, but this method can be hard work and inevitably takes off some metal. It can be mechanized to some extent by using an electric drill and an emery flap wheel, but this will seldom reach into corners, so has limited use for frame and fork work. Always let the tool do the work and do not force it along.

The same rule applies to alloy polishing, which may be called for on fork crowns or legs. It can be done by hand, but more normally is by powered mops, which need using with care. They need plenty of power to drive them and can round off edges or draw holes all too easily, so use with caution.

Hand polishing is done with wet-or-dry

BSA Sunbeam scooter with one-sided front forks, having tube and damper units side by side in the single leg

emery cloth, used with paraffin, and is a tedious and dirty job. You will need medium grade and two grades of fine to achieve a good finish, and the major areas can be done using a Loyblox, which is a block of rubber impregnated with emery grit and can be used wet or dry. A final polish can be given using Solvol Autosol or Belgom Alu, applied with a soft cloth.

Remember that steel parts will rust if left unprotected, so they must be etch primed if the final finish is paint, or greased if they are to be plated.

Repairs and replacements

These are likely to involve the bearings and bushes, suspension units and springs, threads and studs, brackets, damaged tubes or sheet metal, and alignment. Many can be dealt with

ABOVE **Kawasaki KR500 road racer with monocoque body form incorporating the fuel tank with riveted side panels**

BELOW RIGHT **Special with cast alloy backbone frame and rear fork, Norton engine and nice finish**

using basic hand tools, while others will need either welding gear or a butane torch to warm up parts before they are straightened. Damage is likely to call for welding, while alignment problems often have to be farmed out.

Threads and studs have already been discussed, while brackets usually only need heating and straightening, or some welding, to correct splits and cracks or repair an elongated mounting hole. This last would be built up and then filed back to shape to match the rest of the part.

Damaged sheet metal may often be repaired in a similar manner, but invariably this will need welding gear. Some work with sheet metal will call for dollies and a mallet to reform a bent or dented area, and for this some experience is necessary. Tin bashing, as it is often called, is an exact skill and one not easily or quickly acquired, so practise before attempting a simple repair and farm out the complex ones.

Minor damage to tubes can often be repaired using a hacksaw, file and welding gear, but even the most minor damage needs to be thought out first. Anything more major will call for more extensive surgery, and a common repair method is to cut out the damaged section

and replace it. If a sleeve is used at each joint, it will retain its strength, and usually brazing and pinning will hold the parts together, but only if they are truly clean when you join them.

The problems of checking and correcting frame alignment will be looked at further in a later chapter, as will dealing with the various bushes and bearings associated with the frame and forks. Suffice to say that, as always, they need to be cleaned, examined and replaced if worn, these tasks being carried out with care and in the correct manner.

Finishing

Before this can be done, the surface of the part must be prepared, as its condition will be reflected by the final outer surface. All pit marks will show through, unless they are removed, and if the part is to be plated, a resin filler cannot be used.

First, an assessment of the strength of the item must be made, especially with vital items such as the frame and fork legs. With old machines, it is common for the main members to be well pitted or corroded and, hence, too weakened for further use. Do not be deceived by a fine paint finish, for if applied over a thick layer of filler, it will have limited strength. Remember, more than one downtube has parted while the machine was being wheeled about.

The next step depends on the size of the part, as a small or heavy-section part can have any pits filed or polished out. For items such as frame tubes this is not practical, and for these the pits should be filled with a resin filler applied in several coats. Once it has hardened it can be rubbed down with wet-or-dry, used wet, until a smooth, even surface has been obtained, but do not delude yourself; if there is a mark, it will show through every coat of paint you apply.

Most plating has to be farmed out, although nickel plating can be done at home. Select your plater with care, discuss the work with him and do as much of the expensive, labour-intensive polishing and preparation as you can. A number of fork parts will normally be chrome plated, and this may well include the top nuts, but smaller fastenings will be either cadmium or zinc plated. Ensure that all threads are clear and run together without binding after they have been plated.

Painting

Painting can be done by hand or with a spray-gun, although the latter method tends to be expensive of paint when dealing with a tubular frame, as so much of it finishes on the back wall. Some spray paints are dangerous and give off a lethal vapour, so are not for the amateur at all. Check very carefully if you go down this road, but avoid it unless you have full knowledge, all the correct equipment, take all safety precautions and have a fire extinguisher to hand. Modern, air-drying brush paints will produce an excellent finish if applied with care, the correct brush and under reasonable conditions. Some restorers work wonders with an aerosol, although many will be needed, but most prefer the brush.

A synthetic enamel is the popular choice and may simply come in a tin or as a two-part pack. With the latter, one part acts as a hardener to reduce the drying time, and it may be feasible to low-temperature bake the finish. Read the instructions first and remember that preparation, a clean painting environment and care are the keys to a good finish, not the paint type.

A major problem for the home restorer is dust and flying insects, but these can be reduced by keeping to the rules. Some of these are paint after rain has washed the dust out of the air; choose a warm, still day and damp down the work area before you start; avoid woollen gar-

ments or any that can harbour dust; avoid draughts and keep the door shut once you begin; allow some ventilation so that you can breathe, but don't do this on the work; hang it up on wire rather than string, with the least important area facing upwards; use a tack rag before you start and leave the area as soon as you have finished.

A good brush is essential, and most people seem to prefer a Hamilton, which should be run in on something unimportant. Wash any dirt out with several stages of clean paraffin and avoid touching the bristles with your hands or any rag. After the paraffin, wash the brush in warm, soapy water, then clear water and leave to dry.

Do not put the brush into the paint tin, but pour the paint into a clean cup and work from that. Load the brush and apply with a long flowing stroke, allowing the brush to run down the part under its own weight to avoid marks. A good finish will reflect your light touch.

Expect to apply two or three coats and to rub down the surface of each using 500-grade wet-or-dry, used wet, before the next goes on. This will smooth the surface and will also make it easier to see where the next coat must be applied, as this is not always obvious with a dark, gloss surface.

Most frames and forks are painted black, which makes colour matching no problem, but there are exceptions. To match a colour, you really need an original sample that has been shielded from the light, although many common model colours are now known and already matched by paint suppliers.

An alternative to paint is plastic or powder coating, which is tough, but without quite the high level of gloss of paint. Small items can be done at home, but a frame would need to be farmed out and, as always, a talk with the firm first will pay dividends, as they can advise on preparation and what to do for the best results.

A few frames have been nickel plated, with Rickman being perhaps the best known, and this gives an excellent finish. The major problem lies in the plating operation, as it is essential that either the tube interior is totally sealed or that it is washed out fully and drained. If this is not done, the plating solution will cause corrosion and trouble.

Lining and transfers

Modern frames are simply painted with, maybe, a transfer or two, or a serial data plate, applied to them. In the past, they were sometimes lined as well, and for most of us the solution to this task is to farm it out. It is a job which must be done well or not at all, as any imperfection will be painfully obvious. One aid is a car lining tape which has a removable centre strip which, thus, leaves two outers equally spaced as a mask.

Do not forget that the lining paint must be of the same type as that to which it is applied, otherwise they may react. Remove any masking tape you use before the paint has dried fully, as the tape may lift the edges of hardened paint. Gold lining will need to be protected with a clear coating, and yacht varnish is a favoured solution.

Apply the transfers according to their instructions and in the correct position. They, too, will benefit from a thin coat of clear varnish once in place and dry. Most can now be obtained from the Vintage Motor Cycle Club transfer scheme, which is available to non-members and well advertised in the specialist press.

Hard chrome plating

This is a process often used to reclaim fork tubes, but can also be used on worn shafts in general. It deposits a good thickness of material which can then be ground back to size, so is eminently suited to fork legs and plunger columns.

As with metal spraying, another commercial means of reclaiming worn items, care with the preparation and use of the correct technique will ensure a good job. If this is not done, there may be problems with flaking, which would damage other parts.

Modifications

These can range from adding a bracket to major alterations to frame or forks, the substitution of another engine in place of the original, or even the construction of a frame from bare tubing. They include the addition of a sprung rear end to a rigid frame, although this is seldom done now, while the converse happens more often in the chopper and custom

fields to produce the 'hardtail'.

Regardless of what the change is, it must be carried out with due regard to engineering standards and its effect on the basic layout of the complete machine. A change of forks should first be checked for the resultant rake and trail, while a change of engine can have many repercussions.

Just about anything can be carried out if you have the facilities, ability and know what you are about. If you have any doubts on any score, double-check before you start and have the work looked over by an expert after all is complete. It is rather like scrutineering at a race meeting, where a casual glance is not good enough and each aspect has to be looked at with care.

Detail lining on front fork tubes of this early machine shows what may be required on all frame members

ABOVE **Wasp frame kit, which shows the fittings, engine plates and other details involved with the frame and forks**

CHAPTER 3
Bushes and bearings

All machines have some means of pivoting the front wheel from the frame, and for the vast majority this means head races. Even the exceptions have this facility in some way, so retain the races, albeit in a different form. Bushes and bearings can also be found in all suspension systems and, while most allow rotary movement, those used in telescopic forks and rear plungers have a linear travel.

The quality of bushes can vary a good deal, the worst running steel on steel with grease added more in hope than belief. Better models have bronze or brass bushes, while others can use plastics, needle races or taper-rollers. All need cleaning and checking, replacement being the usual remedy if wear exceeds the limits.

Rubber bushes are also used as bearings, for they offer movement without the need for lubrication and enough rigidity for most applications. They can still deteriorate and may be destroyed by fire, but are often difficult to remove. Most other bearings fail due to lack of lubrication rather than wear, and often this is through neglect or because a grease nipple or hole is blocked. Another good way to ruin bearings is to use grease when oil is the prescribed lubricant. This applies equally well to AJS, Matchless and Norton Commando pivoted rear forks.

LEFT **Biflex girder fork with a good selection of bushes for renovation**

RIGHT **Taper-roller races, as found in the better headstock and also in some pivoted forks**

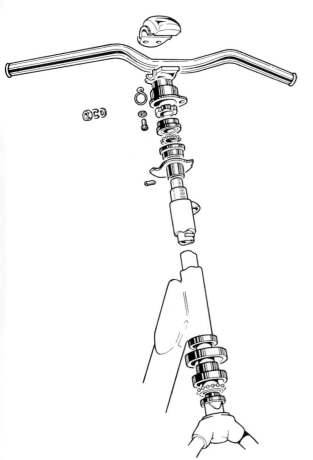

Head races

Early machines, with their bicycle origins, used the cycle's cup-and-cone race with loose ball bearings, and this type is still common now. It has been made heavier and uses larger balls than in the past, but the detail parts are just the same.

Some machines have the balls carried in a simple cage, as this aids assembly, and it may be important that the cage is fitted the right way up. The bearing type is seldom overloaded by the weight it has to carry or the impacts it sustains, but a more precise bearing used by many models is the taper-roller. These have become more common in recent years and are often fitted by owners as a replacement for the original cup-and-cone type.

The Norton Commando, from 1971 onwards, differed from the rest by using conventional sealed ball races for the steering head. These worked very well, despite the end load, as it was impossible for the owner to overload them when adjusting, while the seals kept the grease in and the weather out.

LEFT **Lambretta headstock, which is typical of the scooter type and based on the bicycle form**

ABOVE **Close-up of the lower end of the OEC fork, showing its bearings**

LEFT **The strange front end of the OEC, showing the four-bar linkage that holds the front wheel**

For the unconventional, the head races can be replaced by some form of kingpin, about which the wheel pivots. One of the earliest examples was the Ner-a-Car, which used a short pin and bushes as a pivot for the hub and dispensed with a front brake, which simplified the hub. Much later, post-war, designs tend to use wishbone layouts with car-type ball joints to support the hub spindle, but all suffer from problems with steering lock, the need for a steering linkage and brake anchorage. Proponents of the type claim many advantages, but so far they have failed to impress the buying public, so few will come into the restorer's field. If one does, then its bushes and bearings will need the same attention as any other.

The hub centre design retains the single-axis pivot point of the normal motorcycle, but there was one make that offered something else. This was the duplex steering system that OEC used from 1927 to 1940 as an alternative to normal front forks for those who desired it.

This is not easy to envisage, but from the rider's viewpoint, looking down at the front wheel, there would be a pivot point on each side of the machine in the frame. Each pivot would have an arm extending forwards and inwards a little, with a second pivot at its forward end. These were joined by a cross-member, which carried the front wheel. As the side arms were moved, the wheel turned from one side to the other. For stability, the pivots and arms were duplicated top and bottom, the lower ones being attached to extensions of the lower duplex engine rails. Tubes and spindles ran between each set of pivots, and the whole assembly was laid back at the steering-head angle. The wheel supports were able to slide on their spindles under the control of springs, which provided the front suspension.

The system made for an odd ride with heavy steering, a great deal of self-centring action and no feedback from the road, but worked well enough for those who enjoyed it. The races at top and bottom of the four spindles acted as the head races and would need the same attention as any other.

Servicing head races

This means dismantling, cleaning, inspecting,

33

ABOVE **Feeling for play in the head races of a Triumph; a test needed by all machines**

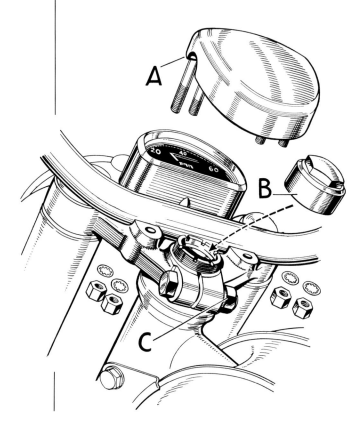

replacing if necessary, assembling and adjusting. The last is often the most important and can affect the machine's handling and determine the head-race life.

Before the races themselves can be dealt with, in most cases it will be necessary to dismantle much of the front end. It may be feasible to change the races without completely detaching the bars, forks and headlamp from the machine, but it can be an awkward job and one fraught with the possibilities of parts being damaged. On a major restoration, the matter will not arise, as items that would be in the way will be removed as a matter of course.

This will leave the forks themselves, and either the legs can be removed one by one or together with the bottom crown. Girder forks differ and are normally dismantled to leave the crowns, while the leading- and trailing-link types may well differ again. Any steering damper will also need to be detached.

The preliminary work will leave the fork crowns ready for attention, and there will commonly be two nuts involved on the steering stem. One will be the locknut and the other the adjuster, but they often are of dissimilar forms. They may be found on either side of the top crown or, in a few cases, beneath the lower one. The second nut may be a threaded sleeve, as is common on many post-war BSA models, but its function will be just the same. Often, the top crown will be slotted and have a clamp bolt to lock it to the stem. This must be released first.

Expect, then, to undo the locknut, slacken, and remove if necessary, the clamp bolt and then undo the main adjuster. You may need to lift away the top crown first but, before turning the adjuster too far, arrange to hold the bottom crown in place. If you do not, all the balls will fall out on to the floor, which is not a good idea, even if they are to be replaced.

Once the adjuster and top crown are clear, you should be able to hold the top race in place and pull the bottom crown and stem away. As it comes away, it will release the lower set of balls, if you have cup-and-cone bearings, so be prepared for them. Hopefully, your data will

Steering head adjustment on many BSA models is with this sleeve nut, which is clamped and locked once set

tell you how many and what diameter are used in each race, but it may not or you may find an error made by a previous owner.

With the lower race clear, check for balls stuck in the bottom cup and then remove the top race. The parts should be washed clean with a solvent and carefully inspected. The procedure is much the same where taper-rollers or caged balls are used, except that they should not fall out, unless the cage is damaged.

Expect to renew the ball bearings and be careful to note the number in each race and their diameter. It is quite common for there to be a variation in both quantity and size, so don't be caught out by this. Wear on taper-rollers is less easy to detect, but feeling for the manner in which the assembly moved, prior to dismantling, should have given some indication, and a close inspection of the rollers may help. If grey and dull, they are most likely worn and in poor condition, in which case, the whole race will need to be renewed. The inner and outer bearing tracks of a roller race will show the same grey, dull areas if worn, but will be shiny and bright otherwise. Still, check for cracks and any signs of chips or damage.

The most likely causes of damage to ball bearing cups and cones is either corrosion, due to the weather, or indenting, due to incorrect adjustment or overloading. Indents can make the machine quite unpleasant to ride, as the forks will try to stay in the position governed by them. The only answer is new parts.

Changing the cups and cones, or the inner and outer of a taper roller, can be easy or difficult depending on the detail design of the items. In general, the top cone or inner roller will be easy as it should simply lift out. The other three items may require more effort, as they should be a tight fit in the headstock or on the stem. Only in a few cases will the cups be fitted into conical housings so that they can be easily lifted or prised out.

The one on the stem can normally be moved by using a small chisel to start it away from its position, followed by a drift. It is essential to work from side to side to keep the cone as near square as possible, and most will be tight for only a short distance, as much of the stem will have a slightly reduced diameter. This also makes replacement easier but, again, the cone must be kept square, and a long tube will help when pressing the new part into place. Make quite sure that no paint, swarf or dirt get under

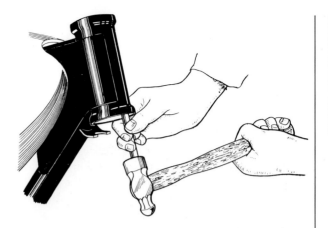

Driving the top cup out of the frame with a drift bearing against its edge, where this is available

the race and that it is completely home. Do not hammer or press on the working surface, but keep to the inner part of the cone, otherwise you may chip or crack it.

The cups may be easy to remove, depending on their inner diameter and the bore of the headstock. If the former is smaller than the latter, you can easily drift the cup out from the other end of the headstock. The only point to watch is that the cup is kept square as it moves.

Should this method not be open to you, the cup ought to have a thread cut into its bore so that a piece of threaded bar can be fitted to it. This will give you something to drift against and the problem will be solved. When there is no thread, it becomes much more difficult.

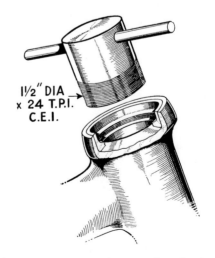

Tool for BSA race cup with screw thread, which is fitted and then driven out together with the cup

One solution is to drill two small holes through the headstock so that a pin-punch can be used to drive the cup out. The holes need to be in the right place and drilled with care, as it is easy to break a drill in the process. Blank off the holes afterwards, otherwise the weather will get in sooner or later to corrode the new bearing.

The final answer, if all else fails, is to grind into the race until it cracks, after which it will come out. It is a tedious job and, inevitably, you will cut into the race housing, but it will get the part out. For some models, there may be a professional tool for the job, but it will be expensive, difficult to obtain and unlikely to be of any use for any other task you ever perform. The choice is yours, but remember that a specialist dealer may be able to help, as may the owner's club, so it is worth checking.

Generally, fitting new cups is easy, but they must go in squarely, with the same strictures on cleanliness as for the cone. Again, any drift must bear against the outer diameter and be clear of the bearing surface to leave this free of distortion or damage. If the cups or cones are loose, you will have a different problem, but one which you must solve and, for once, Loctite is unlikely to be of much help. It may cope with the circumstance of the cup or cone just not being tight, but for anything more is unlikely to withstand the loads imposed on it.

Fitting a new cone on to a steering stem using a tube to drive against the inner part to avoid damage and keep the cone square

The answer is that either the race or the frame will need a small adjustment to their dimensions to enable them to fit together once more. Plating may work on the cup or cone, but the running surface will need to be masked off, and the potential increase in the size of the part would be limited.

If machining facilities are available, it may be feasible to bore and sleeve, but the job is likely to be tricky. It may be possible to cut away the cup housings and make up new ones that will press into place, but check everything by drawing and calculation before you cut metal. In some instances, it is possible to shrink the cup housing by heating the frame and using a blacksmith technique, but it takes skill. The housings will need careful machining afterwards and the alignment may be disturbed, so it would need checking.

Head race adjustment

Once the cups or outer races are firmly in position in the frame and the bottom cone or inner race on the steering stem, the parts can be assembled and adjusted. There may be an oil or grease seal to include, which should be replaced, and the assembly will need to be greased—in fact, this will be essential with loose balls to hold them in place.

For most machines, the procedure is to pack the top balls into the cup and add the cone. Then position the lower balls in grease on the bottom cone and thread the stem up through the headstock and top cone. While doing this, it is important to ensure that the top race is not disturbed and that none of the lower balls is displaced. If either occurs, you will have to start again.

It is also important to make sure that you have the right number of balls of the correct diameter in each race. They may be the same top and bottom, but often differ in both size and number, while it is easy to assume you need one more than you really do. This is because there will be a space approximately equivalent to the size of one ball left to allow the set to revolve in use, and it is all too easy to think you have to fill it up. Don't do this, otherwise the bearing will wear.

RIGHT Greasing the head races with a rag over the nipple to help the grease reach the right place

Once the stem is in place, add the top crown or first nut, whichever comes first, then the other item and the locknut. You are now ready to adjust the races and stand a better chance of indenting them than at most other times. It may be desirable to assemble some parts of the forks at this stage in order to hold the crowns in line and, if so, it is important that these do not impede any of the adjustments.

The adjustment is easy to get wrong, as many machines offered to the press for testing have shown, for too many roll away from an importer with tight races. Not only do they suffer from this low-speed impression, but they will indent quickly and soon wear out. If slack, the same thing happens, because the parts can move about. Therefore, the trick is to remove all slack but without causing tightness. At this happy point, the forks will move smoothly and freely from lock to lock without any trace of stiffness.

The common mistake to avoid is to run the adjuster down until the race is just right, hold it at that point and tighten the locknut. What happens is that the adjuster is forced down on its thread, and this movement is just enough to ruin the races. Thus, you need to back it off a little and then lock it up, bearing in mind that tightening it too much once is once too many.

So, set it at least half a turn back and see how it takes up. Close it up a trifle at a time until it has a precise feel. If set straight ahead, it should stay still, but when moved a few degrees, it will fall over to full lock. If it goes tight on the way, something is bent or the races have not been fitted squarely.

Owners of 1971-onwards Norton Commandos are spared all this, as they have sealed ball races, so all that is necessary is to tighten the nut. This clamps on the inner races only, so there is no adjustment, and the seals keep the grease in and the weather out.

Girder fork bushes

Dealing with wear in this area is never an easy task, as the bushes are long, thin and fragile, while their bores need to be finished to a precise, in-line diameter. The situation is even more of a problem where the manufacturer dispensed with bushes on the grounds of economy, or lack of knowledge, and, in either case, some engineering facilities are likely to be needed.

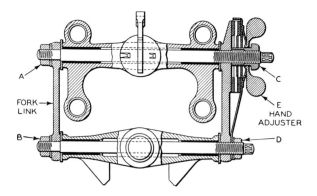

Section through Velocette girder forks, showing the bushes, spindles and friction damper

The first problem with the bushes is their removal, as they may distort or split rather than come out under the action of press or hammer and drift. In really stubborn cases, it may be necessary to either machine them out or to cut through them with a small chisel, with due care for their housings in both cases. It may then be necessary to lightly ream out the fork holes to clean them up, but do not be surprised to find that a previous owner has been there before. It is common to find that all the holes differ in diameter and, thus, special bushes will have to be turned up.

The material to use is phosphor-bronze, and the bushes should either be a light interference fit so that they press in without collapsing, or a hand push fit so that Loctite can be used to hold them. Avoid driving the bushes into place, as this is sure to damage or distort them due to their thin wall. Once they are in place, they will need to be reamed to suit the spindles which, no doubt, will also have had to be replaced. Reaming is important, but not easy, unless you are lucky enough to have the special tool with a pilot. Do not forget to provide the lubrication holes, slots or grooves at some stage before reaming, and always remember how little material there is to play with.

This last aspect is the real trouble where no bushes were fitted originally. In the main, the wear will normally be to one side, so even cleaning out to a diameter on the original centre can be a tricky machining job. A judgement then has to be made as to whether the fork can be bushed and still leave enough wall thickness for the loads it carries. The same problems can afflict attempts to make oversize spindles. This is always a tricky job that must not be attempted without due thought as to the safety of the result when in use.

General bushes and bearings

These are much less of a problem as most are easy enough to replace if worn. New parts will have to be made from scratch in many cases so, once again, possession of a lathe will make all the difference.

Most bushes will be made from phosphor-bronze and can be simply pressed out and in. Lubrication holes or other requirements must not be forgotten and, in general, it is necessary to ream to size after the bush has been installed. Again, this should present no problem to those with the equipment or suitable engineering contacts, but otherwise it is a job to farm out.

Bushes may be made from plastic, nylon often being popular, as it can be moulded from a self-lubricating grade. Try to keep to original mouldings as replacements, if you can, because machined ones seldom have the same texture and may not wear in the same way.

The wear problem should not arise with rubber bonded bushes, which have an inner and outer tube with the rubber in between. Such bushes are used at the ends of suspension units and may also be found in rear fork pivots and other applications of limited angular travel.

The bushes do not wear, but the bond can break, which leaves the problem of removing the old pieces and fitting the new bush. Once more, a lathe can help in making suitable tools to enable the items to be pressed out and in, but without these aids, the task may be less easy. The outer is a thin steel sleeve and, while it can be cut out with a small chisel, this must be done with care to avoid damage. Fitting can be equally awkward, unless something can be found to press on the outer rather than the longer inner portion. Very occasionally a socket spanner will do the job, in which case it all becomes easy with the aid of a bench vice.

Bearings may be of the needle or taper-roller type and usually have a very long life if correctly lubricated—and a really short one if not! Wear means replacement, and a needle race should be pressed out and in with a new inner sleeve for it to bear on. Taper-rollers need to come out and enter square to their bores, and

Leading-link forks with bushes at rear and dampers hidden in pressings

their adjustment is critical. In some cases, they may be pre-loaded, so consult your manual and follow the steps with care.

Telescopics and plungers

These both have bushes with a linear movement, rather than the usual rotary one, but require the same treatment as any others. The telescopic bushes have the benefit of the damping oil acting as a lubricant in many cases, but not all.

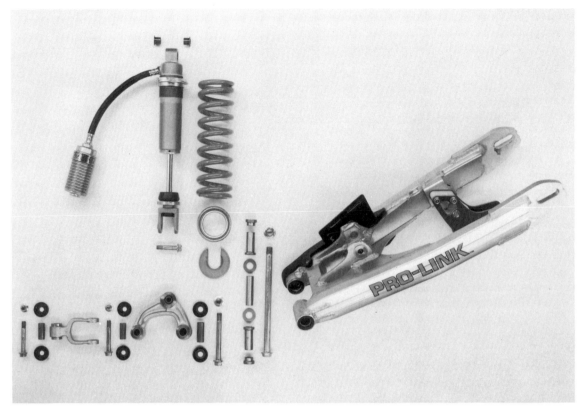

ABOVE The parts of the Honda Pro-link system, all of which need attention at regular intervals

BELOW The Dunlop front forks of the post-war Watsonian motorcycle, which used rubber as the suspension medium

Where the forks rely on grease, they are as likely to be neglected as plungers, with the same results of wear and corrosion. Replacement is the usual answer, employing a press or draw-bolts to withdraw the old and insert the new, after which reaming is likely to be needed.

Unbushed parts can bring the same problems as girder forks, and the same solutions can apply, which means a need for engineering facilities and some careful work. Some telescopic forks may have one bush that can be replaced, but not the other, and this, too, can be tricky to restore, even with good equipment.

Maintenance

The major lessons to learn, from all of the above, are that adjustment can be critical and lubrication is essential. If you experience real trauma in repairing the bushes and bearings, you are unlikely to forget any of this, which could be a good thing.

Make quite sure you remember for the future, as well-lubricated, unworn bushes will prevent all the tricky problems and ensure better handling and steering.

CHAPTER 4
The frame

The frame can come in one of many forms and may be a massive item or a minimal one. It can be made from tube or sheet, be brazed, welded or pressed, be one coherent part or a bolted structure, and be constructed from steel, aluminium or a combination of both.

Its purpose is to act as the structure which supports the engine, gearbox and other working components, along with the rider and passenger, while keeping the front forks and rear wheel in their designed positions. To do this, it must be strong enough to withstand the loads imposed on it. This strength may be provided by the design of the frame alone or augmented by the use of the engine unit as a stressed member.

The loads on the frame are generated by the weight it carries, the road shocks passed via the wheels and suspension, the torque reaction of the engine itself and the pull from the transmission. Braking can introduce further loads, some in the opposite direction to those produced by the driving force.

The frame is designed to cope with all this for a long period, with due allowance for manufacturing discrepancies and owner neglect. If it is in a reasonable condition and all the mountings are assembled correctly, it should continue to function without any problems. Where this is not so, there could be cause for concern.

One of the reasons for trouble can be corrosion, and it must be remembered that this can occur on the inside as well as the outside of tubes, lugs or sheets. The material may also be brittle and, if there is any doubt, renovation

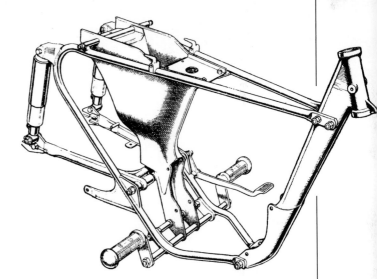

Combined tubes and pressings built up for a Francis-Barnett Cruiser, the downtube being a welded fabrication

will be necessary if the machine is to be ridden. That last caveat is included, as some machines are restored purely for show. If you acquire such a machine and intend to ride it, be extra careful in checking all load-bearing members to ensure that they are up to their job. Do not be deceived by a wonderful finish, as it may be applied over filler, and the steel underneath may be totally unable to cope with modest road loads. The previous ravages of pits and rust, plus blasting to clean the material, can reduce tube wall thickness dramatically, so beware.

The fixings to the frame should be in a reasonable condition and neither cracked nor

ABOVE Perhaps the best known post-war frame in its most classic form; the Norton Featherbed with a Manx engine

BELOW Classic Seeley frame, housing a Matchless G50 engine between its nice, straight tubes

distorted, while past repairs need to be examined with a critical eye. Unless carried out correctly, they may suggest that you should not risk riding the machine. View any modifications you find in the same light, along with any you intend to add. When doing this, remember your intended use, as this can have a great bearing on what you do.

The checks, work-style and approach will vary considerably, depending on whether the machine is to be restored for show, occasional rallies, daily use, touring or competition, since each of these will place different demands on the parts. All, except perhaps in the first instance, must be carried out to a safe standard, but the actual needs of a classic road racer are not the same as the rallyist.

Tube-and-lug frames

These are legion, the earliest being based heavily on the bicycle with its diamond layout. This had to be strengthened to cope with greater speeds and loads, and evolved with time, but the way in which it was made remained much the same well into the post-war era.

The traditional tubular frame was built in a number of types and soon moved away from its bicycle origins, although the pedals remained for some time. Without them, the engine could be mounted low down, just aft of the front wheel, and, later on, the gearbox tucked in behind it. This arrangement developed into the diamond frame, which was often built in two main sections plus separate engine and gearbox plates, all the parts being bolted together. The crankcase of the engine acted as a stressed frame member, and while the result lacked much lateral stiffness, it served the industry well for a long time.

A typical diamond frame has a front section comprising top, down and seat tubes brazed into suitable lugs. The top tube runs from the top of the headstock back to the saddle lug, and is normally braced by a second tube beneath it. This runs from the base of the headstock to the saddle lug to produce a strong, triangulated assembly to hold the headstock in its design position. Do not be dismayed to find that the lower top tube, or tank rail as it is sometimes called, is bent or has a flat in it. This is often done to provide clearance for the cylinder head and can even be present on a side-

valve model if its frame is common with an ohv version.

The downtube normally terminates in a lug, to which the front engine plates will be bolted. The seat tube runs down to a similar lug for the rear engine, or gearbox plates, but these are usually much larger than the front ones. This is so that they can extend back to carry the gearbox, as well as supporting the crankcase, and also attach to the rear frame section.

This last comprises tubes on each side of the rear wheel, the pair running from the saddle lug to the rear fork ends being known as the seat stays. Below them, chain stays run from the fork ends to the gearbox plates, or further

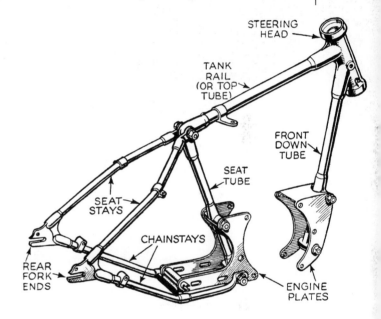

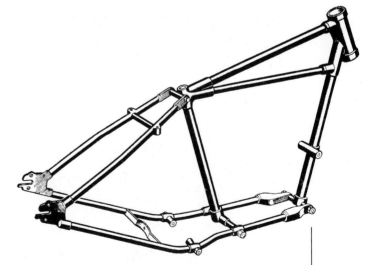

Tube-and-lug frames; the diamond type at the top and cradle above

43

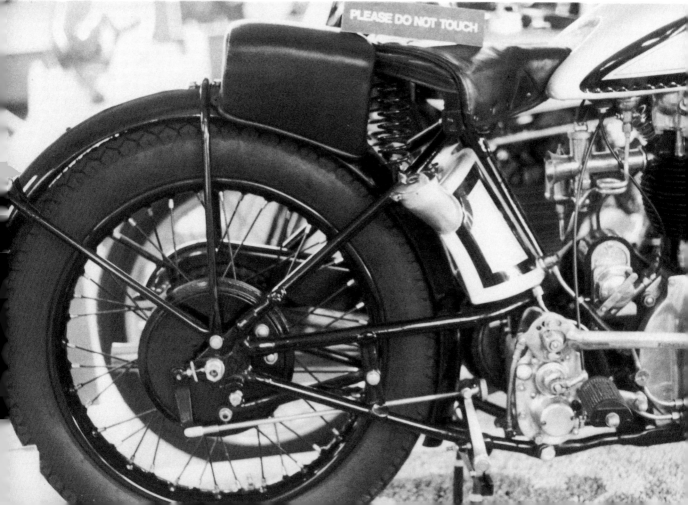

PLEASE DO NOT TOUCH

ABOVE **BSA Star model with forged steel backbone and bolted downtube, as used in the early 1930s**

ABOVE LEFT **Norton cradle frame with plunger rear suspension, known as the 'garden gate', and seen here with International engine**

LEFT **Norton frame with a third chainstay to further brace the rear wheel**

forward to the crankcase area. There are usually cross-stays between each pair of tubes to give the structure rigidity and often to act as the mudguard supports.

In addition to the main frame lugs, into which the tubes fit, there may be others for the brake pedal, prop-stand or other features. Larger machines often have sidecar lugs incorporated in the design; one under the headstock, one at the saddle lug and one near the rear fork ends. A fourth connection is normal, but this will be to the front engine-plate area, which may be adapted to suit.

The above is a description of the basic diamond frame, which works fairly well, but is easily strengthened to become the cradle type. For this, the chain stays are extended forwards to the bottom of the downtube, creating a structure which is no longer dependent on the crankcase for its rigidity. The engine continues to add to this, and to be held in place by plates that also support the gearbox, but is no longer so essential.

A further variation is the addition of a third chain stay, which helps to brace the rear end against side loads generated by the transmission or when cornering. The extreme example of these can be found on older speedway models, which often had a bracing tube added along one side. Without this, there was a good chance of a chain coming off a sprocket, due to the frame whip generated by the combination of engine power and cornering loads.

The cradle frame was lightened for small-capacity models, which often have a loop frame. This differs in having a reduced number of lugs as a result of the tubes being bent. Lugs are used at the headstock and bottom of the seat tube to join the two main sections. Later came the all-welded type, which produced a cheaper, lighter, rigid structure.

45

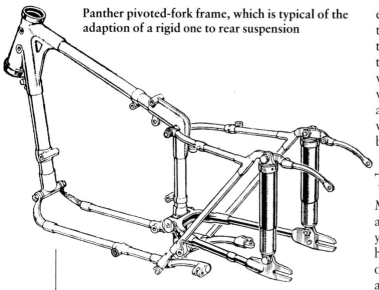

Panther pivoted-fork frame, which is typical of the adaption of a rigid one to rear suspension

For larger machines, the cradle frame may be of the duplex type, but the only difference is that twin downtubes will be used. Often this would be dictated by the engine, and most flat-twins sit in frames of this form.

There are other variations of the basic tube-and-lug frame, each usually being specific to one make. Typical of these was the well triangulated frame used by Cotton during the inter-war period. It had two tubes on each side that ran directly from the headstock ends to the rear fork ends. There was the usual pair of chain stays, plus another above them, a single seat tube and single or duplex downtubes. The result was a very rigid structure that could accommodate a large range of engines.

The early Scott frame also had a considerable degree of triangulation in its layout, in which the engine and transmission main casting played their parts. As with the Cotton, the result was rigidity and precise steering.

A further variant was that used by BSA in the 1930s for their larger machines. This frame had a forged steel backbone, which incorporated the headstock and to which the duplex downtubes and other items were bolted. Although much featured in their advertisements, it was not used after 1936.

A variation of this theme was the use of a fabricated downtube, and this method of construction was employed in pre-war and post-war times with conventional tube-and-lug construction or welded tubes.

An early make that used the frame to carry liquids was the American Pierce of pre-World War I days. This had an in-line, four-cylinder engine in a diamond frame of large-diameter tubes. These comprised top, seat and down-tubes, which also doubled as petrol and oil tanks. Many years later, BSA and Triumph were using frame tubes to house the oil, but where this is done, internal cleanliness is always imperative. Any repairs must be made with this in mind and, of course, the job must be leakproof.

Tube-and-lug frame repair

Minor damage can be fairly easy to put right, as the whole structure is something solid that you can hold in the vice and drill, tap, file or heat up as needed. Threads can be cleaned out or restored with an insert, and bent lugs heated and straightened.

The amount of heat used when making repairs must be tempered with the need to avoid too high a temperature at any brazed lug. This is because it is quite easy to break the steel tube in a lug if the brass around it is molten, so both this and any possibility of causing a crack must be avoided. This proviso must be borne in mind when welding up damaged holes and, if a problem, another solution may have to be sought. This may mean opening up the hole diameter so that a turned collar can be used in it, along with a longer bolt.

Sometimes damaged tubes can be cut so that a new section can be brazed in, along with an internal sleeve. This may not always be easy, and before cutting it is imperative to make notes on hole positions and alignment. Thus, the downtube of a diamond frame can be dealt with in this way, but only if the bottom end returns to its original position so that it can pick up with the engine plates and crankcase.

More serious damage may mean taking the frame apart, and this work calls for a degree of care. The first step is to locate the small pins that peg each tube into its lug and to drill them out. Only then can the joint be heated and the tube extracted, but it is the heat rather than brute strength that will do the job. Any attempt to lever the tube out is likely to snap it off flush with the lug to give a major problem. This may mean using a milling machine, if you have access to one that will reach into the lug recess. The alternative is hard work with rotary cutters, taking care to avoid damaging the lug itself.

Only when the tubes have been removed and

the lug has been cleaned can you proceed further, normally with new tubing cut to size so that the major frame dimensions remain correct. The parts must be really clean before assembly. Then the tubes can be re-pinned into place, with due care being taken over the overall alignment. The brazing is carried out by coating the parts with a paste flux, heating the joint to red heat in the hearth and applying the brass rod, which will melt and run through the joint, provided the temperature is uniform throughout.

The brass is best applied so that it can flow into the joint by capillary action, driving the flux ahead of it, as this will give the best results. It should flow from one end of a joint to the other and not be fed from both ends at once, otherwise some flux may be trapped within the joint. An alternative, which is often used for

blind holes, is to load each with a mixture of brass and flux known as spelter. The joint is then heated until the brass flows to make the joint.

After brazing, each joint will need to be cleaned of scale, which can be done by blasting, and filed to remove any excess. This must not extend into the parent material, as this would result in a stress-raising notch in the tube at just about the worst place. Finally, the frame will need finishing in the usual way, but not before the alignment has been checked.

Post-war Horex with open diamond frame supporting unit-construction engine and gearbox

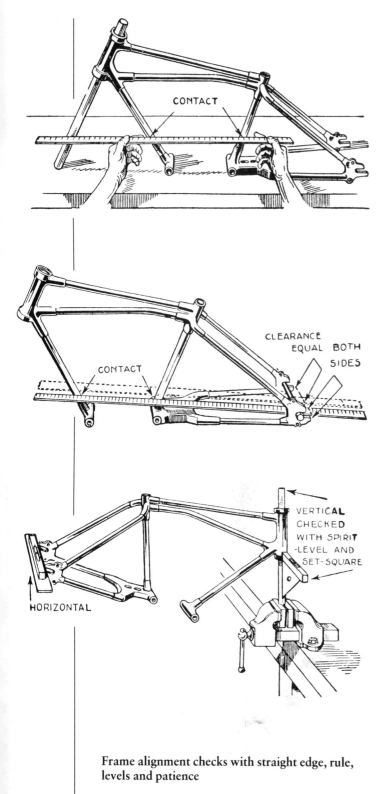

Frame alignment checks with straight edge, rule,
levels and patience

Frame alignment

Modern frames are often checked, and
straightened, in a special jig, which can accommodate a whole range of types for which basic
dimensions and data are available. They may
also be checked by less sophisticated methods,
using straight edge, string, level, rule and
plumb line, plus a good deal of patience.

The basic essential is that the headstock is
square to the rear wheel spindle or rear fork
pivot, and this can be checked with a spirit level
if the headstock is set up vertically. Other
checks can be made along the frame to check
for twist, and most are done by comparing one
side to the other. String or twine makes a good
straight edge and can often give a more accurate answer, as long as it is used with care.

Correcting any errors, other than those
caused by damage, is a task that calls for a
degree of expertise and equipment seldom
found in the normal home workshop. This is
because it will be necessary to hold the frame
securely and be able to heat up considerable
areas at the same time.

Most experts have a vertical bar set in the
floor and mount the frame to this by its headstock. Distance pieces and conical collars
enable it to be held securely and provide a
means by which it can be aligned as required.
The heat source may be a brazing hearth or
one or more torches, for the heat needs to be
spread out rather than localized. Experience
teaches the expert where to apply the heat and
how hard to lean on the frame to move it into
the required shape, but I fear there are no stock
answers or standard rules for this.

With a problem of this kind, it is often best
simply to clean the parts and let the expert deal
with the matter. Unless you know what you
are doing, you are unlikely to restore the frame
to its true form and may well make the job
more difficult for the expert. Above all, avoid
playing a welding torch on one point, as it is
all too easy to produce a kink in the frame with
such localized heat.

Welded-tube frames

These mainly came on to the scene post-war,
but were by no means a universal choice. Once
the technique of mass-production welding had
been learnt, it was adopted quite quickly for
lightweights, where the numbers made it

economically worthwhile, but this was less so with larger machines.

The small-capacity machine's frame is typified by the BSA Bantam, which had a two-part main loop plus two rear loops, all welded together to produce a light, rigid structure. The small James was similar, while others contrived to use a single main loop, rather than the two pieces as on the Bantam.

The welded frame for larger machines came later, and perhaps the most famous is the Norton featherbed, first seen in 1950. This had a full duplex structure with twin top and down-tubes, these crossing over just behind the head-stock. It became the norm, against which most others were measured.

Since then, the use of welded tube has spread to most large machines and, in modern times, the material may be steel or aluminium. All manner of sections are used now, but this is nothing new, for oval, square and fabricated sections have been in use for many years. Square tubing has the advantage to the manufacturer of making it easy to attach brackets and is available as cold-drawn stock,

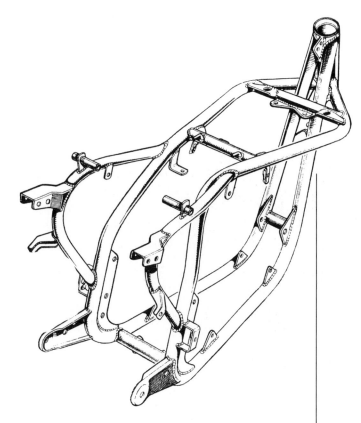

BELOW **Modern Honda VFR750R with aluminium twin-beam frame linking headstock and rear pivot as directly as possible**

ABOVE The Slimline Featherbed frame, which includes all the extra brackets for road use

The Motoliner frame-straightening system for
modern machines of welded construction

but the other types are generally pressed or
formed and then seam welded.

Repair of this type can be more difficult than
the tube-and-lug form, as it is all too easy to
leave an inbuilt stress in the structure after
welding it. This can be proved by cutting
through a tube, as misalignment across the cut
implies a locked-in stress.

Equipment is available for use with modern
frames that can check the critical dimensions
and correct errors using hydraulic rams. Some
restorers are happy to use these systems, while
others decry them, but the answer, as usual,
lies between the two extremes of opinion. The
modern gear can correct the frame, but it must
be used with skill, along lines suggested by
experience. If this is done, then some frames
can be mended this way.

Others may be damaged too much or be in
the wrong place for this equipment to work.
The skill lies in recognizing this and making
due allowance for it. Where this is the case, it
is likely that part of the frame will have to be
cut out to allow the rest to be corrected. Once

this has been done, the removed section can be
replaced, with the joints suitably sleeved to
maintain or improve the original strength.

Pressed-steel frames

These come in as many variants as the tubular
type and have been in use since the 1920s. Most
early examples came from Germany, but some
also appeared on Czech, British and French
machines. In the post-war years, pressed-steel
became the preferred material for the frames
of most mopeds and many small models, while
falling from favour for larger machines. Often,
it was combined with tubular members to form
enclosures or compartments, a practice which
continues to this day.

Pre-war pressed-steel frames were usually
laid out just as their tubular brothers, so they
followed the same outline. There would be one
large pressing on each side, the various tubes
being replaced by steel sheet, the edges of
which were turned in to strengthen it. Often,
this led to a heavy and awkward appearance,
frequently made worse by positioning the fuel
tank between the upper members. Examples of
the type were built by BMW and Zundapp of
Germany, Dresch and Gnôme et Rhône of

ABOVE **Early post-war Laverda with pressed-steel frame and blade girder forks**

BELOW **Raleigh moped with rigid beam frame and bicycle forks to produce the most basic form of transport**

France, and Jawa of Czechoslovakia during the 1930s. The conservative British were less keen on the idea, but Coventry Eagle used the frame type during that decade, as did Francis-Barnett.

Not all followed this pattern, as some altered the design to increase the size of the main member that ran from the headstock to the rear wheel. The engine could be hung from this or further supported by welded-on pressings, which extended down behind the gearbox with bolted-on struts to act as the downtube and chainstays.

This layout was used by DKW back in the 1920s and became familiar in the 1950s, for it was most suited to mass-produced lightweights. The notion of a beam running from one end of the machine to the other, with forks at the front, a wheel at the rear, the engine hung from the middle, and a saddle above, produced the basic moped first epitomized by the NSU Quickly.

This model broke away from the motorized cycle mould and introduced a form that continued for many a year. The two frame halves were pressed and then welded in one operation, cutting production time to a fraction of that normally taken. From the basic type came many variations, but all were based on the spine design, the engine being hung from the frame, rather than installed in it.

A variant is the 'T' frame, the main section of which runs straight back from the headstock, under the fuel tank, to support the dualseat. An extension continues down from this, behind the engine unit to support it and the rear suspension, while a light strut may be bolted in place to act as a downtube.

The configuration works well for small-capacity machines and was also chosen for the Ariel Leader model, introduced in the late 1950s. This had a main beam built up from pressings and welded together in a rather more complex manner, but the principle was the same.

The use of pressed-steel can be extended to include enclosure with the frame construction, but this is less easy to arrange satisfactorily. All too often, it becomes necessary to add external covers, which detract from the appearance, while assembly can be awkward, as can servicing. An early example was the Ascot Pullin, which appeared late in 1928 with all these points and in a similar style to the earlier Pullin-Groom.

ABOVE **Aermacchi Chimera with tubular beam frame and monoshock rear suspension**

TOP LEFT **Italian Motobi with beam frame supporting horizontal engine**

TOP RIGHT **Conventional James Comet with tube and pressed-steel frame, which concealed the forward-mounted rear springs**

Frames can also be made by using folded rather than pressed-steel. Examples are the Royal Enfield Cycar, built for several years in the 1930s, and the post-war LE Velocette, which was similar, but included a small tubular subframe, footboard pressings and a cross bracket in its total frame assembly.

Pressed-steel repairs

These are more akin to mudguards and similar sheet components, with cracks, splits, oversize holes, loose rivets and joint corrosion being the major problems. To deal with all but the simplest will call for welding and some sheet-metalworking skills.

Minor dents can often be tapped out using a suitable weight of hammer and polished dolly, but for anything more than the simplest you should use panel beater's tools. Misalignment and major damage will be less easy to put right, as the former will call for major heating to correct and the latter can result in stretched metal and wrinkles. Again, sheet-metalworking skills and panel beater's tools will be needed, along with a welding torch to allow parts to be cut and rejoined.

Built-up and composite frames

These are mainly either bolted together using a set of small parts or constructed from tube and sheet-steel. Invariably, there are exceptions that fall into other classifications.

A prime example of the built-up frame was that used by Francis-Barnett for a number of models in the period between the wars. It comprised six pairs of straight tubes, plus one pair with a small kink, and these were simply bolted together to form the frame. The tube ends were marked to a plan and assembly took a matter of minutes. One additional odd feature of the construction was that the headstock tube became part of the front forks and turned about a fixed pin, which joined the front ends of the pairs of tank, saddle and downtubes. The assembly was a trifle wide across the junction by the footrests, but the system worked.

If this Francis-Barnett frame was easy to repair by simply replacing a tube or two, the Danish Nimbus was, in some ways, even easier. The frame of that model comprised simple flat steel bars arranged in a duplex form and riveted to the headstock and fork ends. The bars were $1\frac{1}{2}$ in. deep, but only $\frac{1}{4}$ in. thick, so relied on the engine unit to brace them. However, the result was effective enough for the machine's performance. In part, this was due to the weight being low down and the longish wheelbase, dictated by the in-line, four-cylinder engine.

A few machines have used steel channel for their frame members, but this did not produce very good results. The section lacks strength in torsion and can easily fold-up if bent into the channel. It is easy to repair or replace, but has little other merit.

Most composite frames have a tubular front section with a pressed-steel rear section welded or bolted to it. This method was used by a number of post-war James and Francis-Barnett models to produce a neat layout for cheap lightweights. DMW also used this method, as did Japanese manufacturers in later years. Some scooters were built in this manner, too, although most were based on a single, large-diameter tube that ran from the headstock to the machine's rear. Certain panels, or outrigger tubes, could be welded to this to provide the basis of the enclosure and give the structure rigidity.

The spine frame may also be of the built-up type, and this type is commonly found on low-volume, specialized models, usually constructed for some form of competition. One example was the Scorpion, which used a T frame form made from sheet-steel folded to a square section and welded together. This appeared in the 1960s and worked well in trials and scrambles form, but their prototype road racer used a single, large-diameter tube for its spine frame. It was not a new idea, for many road racing specials had used this arrangement in one way or another, while the form was common for sprint machines at one time. The latter were often made from a bus exhaust pipe, as this provided both the required diameter and

Scorpion with frame welded up from folded steel sheets to produce an effective 'T' form

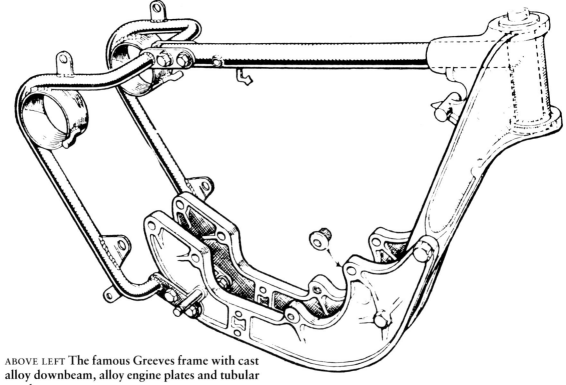

ABOVE LEFT **The famous Greeves frame with cast alloy downbeam, alloy engine plates and tubular rear loop**

a ready-made bend. It could then have the engine hung from it and act as a tank for the minimal amount of fuel needed for the dash up the strip.

A less conventional composite frame was that used by the Greeves firm for many years, as this had a cast alloy front down-member. The frame was constructed by welding the headstock to the top tube, after which the beam was cast to encompass the headstock and the welded joint. This was not the only alloy in the frame, for twin carriers ran from the base of the down-beam, under the engine and up to a small, cast alloy battery carrier. The frame was completed with tube loops that ran from the alloy plates to the rear of the top tube and incorporated the rubber rear units or the suspension pick-up points.

Other firms used combinations of tubes, plates and pressings to construct their frames. For some, this simply meant a fabricated downtube, formed to give depth and strength without too much width to detract from the styling or impede either airflow or an exhaust pipe.

More complex was that of the Norton Jubilee twin, which had pressings and tube loops bolted together under its rear enclosure panelling. The Italian Moto Guzzi firm was also fond of bolted frame construction for its racing machines, and many had tubes, lugs, forgings and plates bolted or riveted together in a highly characteristic and successful style.

Monocoque and minimal frames

These might be referred to as 'all or nothing', for the former includes frame, panelling, housings and often the fuel tank in its single structure. The latter, however, is an attempt to reduce the frame to a minimum by using the engine structure as a stressed member to carry suspension loads.

The Ascot Pullin, already mentioned, was an early attempt at a monocoque frame, and there were others. One of the oddest was the German Megola, which had a fabricated beam frame, in which the main fuel tank was incorporated. Even more odd was the use of a five-cylinder radial engine, built into the front wheel, and semi-elliptic rear springs.

There was also the French New-Motorcycle of the late 1920s, which had a sheet-metal frame, into which the engine and gearbox were

ABOVE RIGHT **Vespa scooter with pressed-steel chassis, from which the complete engine and rear wheel unit pivots**

RIGHT **Pre-war MGC with cast alloy frame members and bolted construction**

bolted, effectively out of sight, with the head-stock and enclosing rear mudguard riveted into place. The post-war Piatti scooter was much smaller and had its engine unit tucked completely out of sight under a low monocoque steel body. For most servicing, it had to be laid on its side, but it worked well enough for town transport in the 1950s.

The Vespa scooter had a monocoque chassis built up from pressings, and the strengthening channels were used to conceal both controls and wiring. Thus changing a cable can be something of a problem, but frame repairs are the same as for any pressed-steel item.

One pre-war use of alloy castings was to be seen on the French MGC of the 1930s, which combined the alloy petrol tank, incorporating an instrument-panel recess, with the upper frame members. A further casting went beneath the engine and gearbox, while links and struts were bolted in to complete the assembly. A much earlier example was the American Schickel of the 1910s, which had the headstock and seat post tube formed into the petrol tank ends with a suitable boss for the downtube. A modern version of this construction was used by the 1980 Kawasaki KR500 road racer which, again, had the headstock in the tank front and

some frame members built in, although others were riveted into place.

The idea of using the engine as a major part of the frame is not entirely new, for the 1927 German Windhoff in-line four followed this path. It had the steering head attached to the front of the cylinder head for the front wheel, and struts from the gearbox for the rear wheel. The post-war Vincent followed these lines, with a simple frame member above the engine. This doubled as the oil tank, was bolted to both cylinder heads, had the steering-head lug attached to it by special bolts, and took the loads of the rear spring units and damper.

Most other machines of this type have been built for road racing, where the requirements differ from conventional highway or off-road riding. The engine unit has to be constructed to cope with the added loads, which must be fed into its structure to avoid points of high stress. Engine balance and vibration also play their part, as there can be no rubber insulation and, thus, no isolation from the effects.

One of the more unusual ways of using the engine as a stressed link, between the front and rear frame sections, appeared on the Italian Rumi scooter of the 1950s. It was powered by a 125 cc twin two-stroke engine with parallel,

ABOVE **A 1931 Vincent-HRD featuring the monoshock rear suspension used always by the marque and here with Rudge engine**

ABOVE LEFT **The Honda racing NR500 of 1979 with monocoque frame and limited access to its working parts**

forward-facing cylinders, this unit-construction egg being bolted to cast alloy frame members. There were two main ones at the front, which extended up to form a nacelle and to carry the headlamp in further castings. Incorporated in them were housings for the fork races, and the leading-link forks carried a massive, cast alloy mudguard.

The rear of the machine comprised further castings, the main one being bolted to the rear of the engine unit, where it supported the seat. Thus, it formed the rear body, in which pivoted a single arm to carry the rear wheel and form the inner half of the full rear chaincase. Only the combined legshields and footboards were in sheet metal, and they joined the front and rear castings.

Restoration of this type of frame concerns either the repair of holes and threads, which is fairly easy, or cracks and distortion, which is quite difficult, even with good equipment. This sort of damage should be considered very carefully before attempting any repairs.

Modern frames

During the 1980s frame design moved on, especially for the super-sports and race replica models, which copied works machines in both style and technology. Duplex beam frames, with or without an engine cradle, and in steel or light alloy, are now common.

The beams are built up from pressings, welded together, and the material and fabrication method should be checked out. Some may look like alloy but, in fact, be steel, while others may have less exciting cross-sections for the areas that are out of sight.

Repair of crash damage is likely to call for specialized equipment and skills, but some of the minor details may be easier to deal with. These include the usual fixings and brackets, and much depends on the frame design itself. Where there is a bolt-in section to allow removal of the engine, this must fit precisely, otherwise much of its effect will be lost, so check this area in detail.

CHAPTER 5
Front forks

These have to carry and steer the front wheel, while allowing it to move up and down under the control of the suspension system. The wheel movement needs to follow a prescribed path in order to maintain the steering geometry, and this must remain true under full travel of both suspension systems, harsh acceleration and heavy braking. The fitting of a sidecar introduces additional and varied requirements.

There have been four main types of front fork over the years, with one or two odd arrangements that fall outside the norm. The major types, however, are girder, telescopic, leading-link and trailing-link, which offer different lengths and patterns of movement to the front wheel as it rises and falls.

It is important to distinguish between the suspension type and its medium, along with the position of that medium and the manner in which it is connected to the suspension. Thus, the type often referred to as bottom-link and found on Harley-Davidson, Brough Superior, BAT and Chater-Lea, among others, and viewed as a heavy-duty and superior form, is really leading-link and, thus, the same type as fitted to a Honda 50. The difference lies in the way the links are connected to the springs and braced to each other.

In addition to the four main classes of fork, there were the original bicycle type used by the pioneers, either as they were or in strengthened

LEFT **Brough Superior SS80 with the Castle leading-link forks favoured by the marque** or strutted form. Naturally, these are also found on most cyclemotors, due to the use of the bicycle, and on some cheap mopeds of the late 1950s period. Other additional fork types are the rocking design, which can be considered with the girder form, and the plunger, as used by Wooler and dealt with as the telescopic pattern. The OEC duplex is also really a form of telescopics, while the rest of the hub-centre type are considered as a group on their own, although often conforming to one of the main types.

Early strutted bicycle forks, which offered no suspension and little extra strength from the added tubes

Girder forks

The earliest sprung forks were often of the leading-link type, and the motorcycle was well into its Edwardian era before girder forks made their appearance. The type is characterized by a fork that carries the wheel and is attached to the steering-head yokes by links. It may have a single, central main spring or one on each side, and there are often auxiliary or check springs as well.

The fork itself may be constructed like a

Triumph Tiger 100 of 1939 with its girder forks and their friction dampers

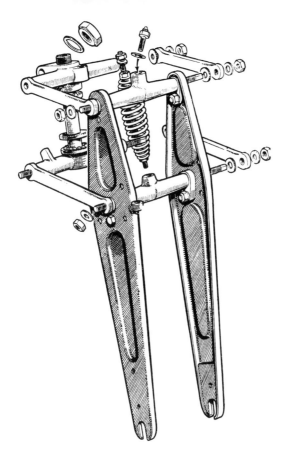

Lightweight pressed-steel blade girders, as used by the wartime James model

frame from tubes and lugs that have been brazed together, but not all follow this basic form, which is sometimes braced with extra tubes on each side. This latter type is known as the strutted version and is better able to cope with side loads, which is more than can be said for blade girders. These were popular for autocycles and lightweights, each fork side being a pressed-steel blade which, thus, offered limited bracing to the other. They were, however, cheap and easy to produce.

A further variant for light machines used a tube on each side, so had the appearance of a telescopic fork, but the action of a girder. Both James and Excelsior used this style in post-war years on low-cost models.

Forks with a single, central compression spring are commonly referred to as the Webb type, although the same form was also made by Brampton and, for that matter, any number of firms for their in-house use. Tension springs were used by some in earlier days, as these simply spanned the gap between the fixed and moving yokes in a different manner but, in

time, the compression spring became the norm.

Early forks often used the alternative of side-mounted springs, with one on each side between the lower yoke and the fork blade, and this type is exemplified by the Druid fork. In time, it fell from favour, and by the 1930s was seldom used. That decade saw more machines fitted with additional check springs, on links extended or modified to give the desired effect, Ariel and Norton being just two examples.

Steel springs in this position were not the only suspension medium used, and the post-war C-series Vincent models used lengthy coil springs in housings that ran from the fork ends up to the lower yoke on their Girdraulic forks. At the other end of the scale, the 125 cc Royal Enfield had a system of rubber bands as its medium, which was taken from a pre-war DKW design. Both Excelsior and Francis-Barnett autocycles of the early post-war period also used rubber bands, and this type has the advantage of an easy adjustment to its suspension load capacity.

The Vincent Girdraulics had forged alloy blades, and their appearance was not unlike that of the wartime Zundapp KS750. These looked like heavy-duty telescopics, but were true girders, the main fork being constructed from welded oval tubing. The fork springs were enclosed within the tubes in the manner of the telescopic fork, but were actuated by rockers connected to the top links.

Girder fork repair

The first step is to dismantle the parts, which is often best done on the machine, as the type does not lend itself to detachment quite as easily as others. It may be possible to remove fork components without disturbing too many other parts, but this is seldom the best way, since it is all too easy for something to slip and either damage itself or another part.

This problem seldom arises with a major restoration, as the peripheral details are the first to come off with a project. It is the odd repair that can lead to mistakes and damage, so start by removing the fuel tank, controls, headlamp and the necessary wiring. This will greatly simplify matters, so the handlebars can be removed and then the speedometer and its drive, the front wheel and front mudguard.

The forks themselves can now be worked on quite easily, so the next item to detach is the

Strutted Druid girder forks with side-mounted springs and limited fork travel

Vincent Girdraulics with central damper and a long spring unit to the rear of each forged alloy fork blade

steering damper. Most of the details should simply unscrew or unbolt, but the lower end of the main spindle is likely to remain trapped by the fork-link spindle and will have to stay where it is for the time being.

The fork spring may be held in place by a variety of methods and should be released when there is the least strain on it. The forks themselves now need the headrace and link nuts slackening, which may then allow the race nuts and top yoke to be removed so that the fork will drop clear of the frame. This will also release all the balls from the headrace.

An alternative may be to remove the links, but be careful on two points. One is to not mix up the links, spindles, nuts or washers, and the

other is to beware of the spring tension. Make sure that the removal of one link will not release, or partially release, the spring, as the former could be dangerous and the latter cause the parts to jam and prevent their dismantling. Your manual should guide you on the exact procedure to follow, but if it does not, think it out first before undoing too much.

The traditional girder fork, built up from tubes and lugs, can be repaired in the same way as a frame, with the same conditions and requirements. It is, perhaps, even more important to check for pits or any other damage, as it is vital that the fork has more than adequate strength for its job. Do not take any chances in this respect.

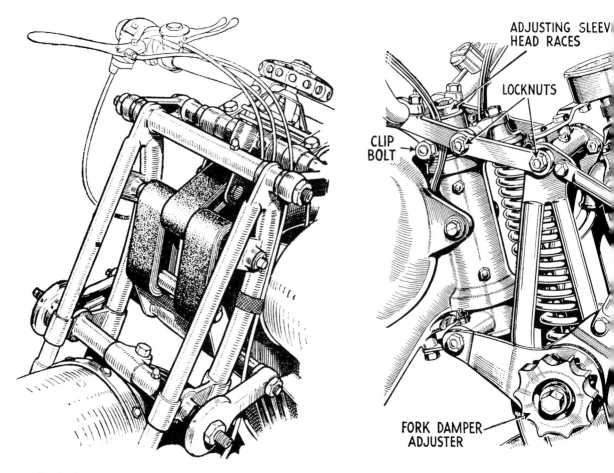

The fork will need to be checked for alignment, and some of this may be done by using mandrels in the spindle holes—preferably after they have been rebushed. Check for twist between the spindles and the wheel slots, and for any signs of bending. Minor adjustments can sometimes be done with the fork cold, but do not expect, or attempt, too much, and be careful of stretching or kinking a tube. If in any doubt, take the fork to a specialist, for it will be your neck at risk when the machine has been completed.

Girder blades or tubes may need similar checks. Blades can usually be heated and restored to shape, but be more careful with tubes, as it is easy to damage them further. Consequently, replacement or a sleeve repair may be a better approach. With either type, check all holes and threads to ensure that they are fit for further service.

Girder links

The links are just as important as the fork itself and need to be examined for cracks, alignment,

worn holes and damaged threads. Each pair should have the same hole centres, otherwise they will throw the fork out, and if you have any thoughts of adopting a policy of 'that's good enough', remember the leverage that the front wheel has over the fork links.

Links commonly have two plain holes for one side of the machine and two tapped ones for the other. While this is the most usual arrangement, there are others that differ and need to be allowed for. Remember also that the link centres govern the trail and that it was common for manufacturers to offer alternative-length links to reduce the trail for sidecar use. Thus, it is best to check the centres if you have to find replacement parts.

Most girder forks simply have the four links, but not all. In some cases, one pair, usually the lower, was designed to act as a part of the friction suspension damper so had a disc incorporated in them. Others had added lugs and holes for check or return springs. These, too, need to be examined and repaired as required.

The design of the BSA girder fork differed from most in that each link was formed with

FAR LEFT **Rubber-band springs**, seen here on a 1935 DKW and also used by the post-war 125 cc Royal Enfield

LEFT **BSA M20 girder forks**, which were typical of the type in most respects, other than the links with integral hollow spindles

RIGHT **Eccentric fork trail adjuster on Vincent Girdraulics**, which moves link centre and preloads spring unit

a hollow spindle at each end. These moved in the bushes in the fork and yokes, with spindles within them to hold them in place and provide a means of adjustment. This makes repair something of a problem as, while it is easy to rebush the holes, it is less easy to deal with wear on the hollow spindles. They can be machined away and new parts made and pressed into place to be secured by brazing or Loctite, but it is a tricky job that must be carried out with precision if the fork is to function properly. Do not attempt it without good facilities and the ability to use them.

Both Rudge and Vincent used one-piece top and bottom links for some models, and these parts are easier to check and correct for alignment. They require the front, solid part of the link to fit between the fork structure, instead of on each side of it, and this may affect the layout of bushes, spindles and washers, as well as their adjustment. If in doubt, consult the manual.

The Vincent models with the Girdraulic fork have this feature and also an eccentric mounting for the lower rear spindle. This is designed so that the pivot centre can be readily moved from one position to another, and the change alters the fork trail from a solo to a sidecar setting. The spring top mounting is incorporated into the eccentric so that its movement also stiffens the spring loading when in the sidecar position.

Fork bushes and spindles have been discussed in an earlier chapter, and associated with them and the links are the spindle nuts and thrust washers. The first must be a good fit with no signs of the thread pulling up. If replacements are needed, make sure they are of a good quality steel. The washers are normally hardened and ground, for they have to take the side thrust and act as an adjustment guide, with at least one on each spindle able to be turned, but without any sideplay.

Girder yokes

The lower yoke is usually formed in one piece with the steering stem, while the upper one may be slotted for a clamp bolt and have the handlebar mountings incorporated into it. Both may

ABOVE Tension fork spring, which was less common and more of a problem if it broke on a journey

LEFT Druid fork spring and its mounting to the fork tube and lower yoke

ABOVE Ariel girder fork with extra check spring arranged to work most on full fork deflection

ABOVE FAR LEFT Typical lightweight forks with central spring on a Norman

be bushed for fork spindles and need to be checked for any signs of damage, cracked or distorted lugs, and poor holes and threads.

The lower yoke will carry the bottom cone on the stem, and the top cone needs to be a good sliding fit at its working position. The stem threads must be in good order, otherwise headrace adjustment will be more difficult than usual, and the underside may be formed to act as part of the steering damper.

Any seals or cups used to exclude the weather from the headstock, or to keep the grease in, must be in good order, as must any grease nipples and their holes. The adjustment

nuts need to be a good, but free-running, fit on the stem, and this is particularly important at the point where they are positioned. If the stem thread is poor in this area, it may be possible to add a spacer and use the unworn thread higher up the stem.

The Francis-Barnett built-up frame differs from others, not only in being constructed from a set of tubes, but in having a fixed steering stem. The headstock revolves around this and incorporates the two yokes to which the links pivot. Assembly and adjustment obviously differs from normal, but is no more difficult.

Girder fork springs

Both tension and compression springs were used in the early days, two being as common as one. The Druid pattern had one compression spring on each side, while the Webb and Brampton, plus many others, had a single, central compression spring. Most latter-day springs were wound in a barrel form to give a rising rate and to enable the springs to be accommodated in the available space. Models with tension springs would usually have two of them, but Triumph models of the late 1920s and early 1930s were an exception, as they managed with a single, central tension spring.

Methods of attachment vary considerably, but a common one is to 'screw' the spring on to a suitably shaped fixing. This may be formed into one of the yokes or fork parts, usually the lower one, or bolted into place. Commonly, the upper one is fixed to the spring and located in a tapered hole, being held by a single bolt. In this way, it is unable to creep round, out of engagement with the spring, but can be released by slackening the bolt a turn or two and then striking its head.

On occasion, it may be found that the spring mountings are arranged to pivot on a cross-pin or in a ball cup. This allows the spring to remain true to its working axis and not be deformed by the fork movement. Such an arrangement must, in the first case, be strong enough to carry the full loads imposed on the mountings and, in the second, be well enough lubricated to enable the spring to self-align, despite the load on the ball and cup.

The design may well include some form of rod and guide bush to help the spring remain in line, while another method is to enclose the spring with pressed-steel covers. In all cases, the parts must be in good order and able to cope with any stress placed upon them. Check springs have already been mentioned, and their action and fastening must be in good order.

All springs must be without wear marks or other indications of significant damage and may need to be checked for signs of weakening. Where they have become shortened, or lengthened in the case of tension springs, replacement is likely to be the only answer, if the parts are available. It may be possible to adapt a spring from another marque or machine, but this must not be done without due thought. The replacement must fit mechanically and

have the desired spring rate so that, when installed, the machine ride height will return to its correct dimension.

Girder fork assembly

Start with the head races; once the cups are in the frame and the lower cone on the steering stem, the yokes can be assembled. The adjustment nut should be run down far enough to prevent the balls from falling out, but not to remove all the play at this point.

The reason for not completing the head race adjustment at this stage is that the two yokes will not necessarily be aligned. Without the forks in place, this would be difficult to control, so the setting should be left slack for the time being, along with any clamp bolt.

Now assemble the spindles and links to the yokes and the fork itself, adopting the procedure set down in your manual. This will also indicate when to add the fork spring or whether to leave this until adjustment has been completed. Again, do not attempt the final adjustment at this point. On many machines, it is imperative to include the steering damper rod at this early stage, as the lower rear spindle usually passes through it.

The exact manner in which the spindles fit into the links can vary, as a number of designs were used over the years. One of the more popular has the spindle threaded into the link at one end and reduced in diameter at the other for a plain link hole. A nut at the plain end effectively pulls the spindle shoulder against the link, while rotation of the spindle winds the threaded link to and fro. This provides an adjustment, and one end of the spindle is normally machined as a square so that it can be turned.

With this type, the plain end locknut has to be slackened before the adjustment can be set and, of course, when this is done, it can allow the link to move out with it. Thus, adjustment must be carried out a little at a time, the locknuts being tightened for each check. Note that the nut at the threaded end must also be tight, as its action will be to pull the spindle in the link thread in the opposite manner to the adjustment. This is a similar situation to that with the head race, and it can produce the same, over-tightened effect.

It is common practice to fit hardened thrust washers between the links and the ends of the spindle holes in the yokes. At the reduced end, the washer must not be allowed to sit on the small diameter, and some care is needed to avoid trapping and, perhaps, cracking it. The washers are often knurled on their edge, and fork-link adjustment will be correct when they have no side-play, but at least one on each spindle can still be turned.

Before this point is reached, the head race adjustment should be taken up, the aim being to draw the spindles and the races to their optimum settings together. If this is done, the parts will be nicely aligned to work freely and precisely.

There are several other methods of assembly to be found, and one of the simpler comprises a long bolt run into the threaded link with a single locknut to secure its adjustment. The BSA design was of this form but, of course, had the spindles incorporated into the links, so the bolts simply provided the means of adjustment and of holding the links in place.

Another method uses left- and right-hand threads on the spindle ends and in the links. These can be a little more tricky to dismantle and assemble, as the two spindles in each pair of links must be turned together. If they are not, the links will tilt and jam. On assembly, both threads at the ends of both spindles need to be started in the link holes at the same time, but this is not as tricky as it might sound.

There are other variations on these methods, but the same basic rules apply, in that the parts must be assembled in the right order and adjusted with some care. All forks require lubrication for the bushes and spindles, the majority being greased via nipples at strategic points. A few use oil and, in either case, an excess is to be avoided, for it can migrate on to both the friction and steering dampers, to their detriment.

Rocking fork on a Precision with leaf-spring suspension and various links to join the pieces

Rocking girders

These are a variation of the girder type and are best known for their appearance on early Triumph models. The fork itself was much the same as a normal girder, but there were no side links, as the fork was pivoted about the lower yoke. This single spindle allowed the fork to move to and fro, with control by a single horizontal spring fixed between the top yoke and the top end of the fork.

Triumph introduced this fork design in 1906,

and it remained in use on some models well into the 1920s. It served in the Great War, and owners and despatch riders all learnt that it was advisable to fit a safety strap round the forks to prevent a total collapse if the spring broke.

The design did not give the best of rides, for the wheelbase changed as the fork moved, but it was better than nothing. The same idea was also used for autocycles, but with just the lower pivot, and control achieved with rubber blocks under compression. An earlier example was

Biflex fork, which can rock as well as rise and fall, but that top front nut must be secure

Rex forks with telescopic action between spring pairs and twin tubes

used by Precision and, in their case, the fork ends were linked to a point above the wheel. A short shackle connected this to an L-shaped leaf spring, which was attached to the head-stock and provided the suspension medium, plus some friction damping. Repair of the rocking fork is much the same as for the normal girder type, comprising a check on alignment, replacement of worn parts and a general inspection for condition.

The main rocking spindle can be bushed or have cup-and-cone bearings and, in either case, these will need to be renovated in the same way

as others of a similar type. The reservations regarding the balls and their number apply as they do for the steering column, likewise the needs of the bearings and their fitment.

A fork which combined the action of the normal girder with the rocking type was the Brampton Biflex. This had tension main springs between the top fork and lower yoke, but there were spring-loaded members in place of the top links. Each still pivoted at the top yoke, but passed through a bush in the fork top with a spring on each side to give the fork a controlled degree of fore-and-aft movement.

It was a design that ran from 1914 into the 1920s, but then disappeared, and is repaired using the methods already described.

Telescopic front forks

The telescopic fork is currently the standard fit on just about all stock motorcycles, with alternatives only being found on mopeds, scooters and specials. The design is often criticized on many engineering counts but it has one great advantage—it works!

The idea of a telescopic arrangement, where the wheel axis moves in a straight line, parallel to the steering head, is not at all new. The Scott is, perhaps, the best known of the Edwardian designs, but Rex is another. More followed, but it was not until 1935 that telescopic forks in their modern style with hydraulic damping appeared on two BMW models. These were the first production machines to have such a feature, although the Danish Nimbus of the same year was also fitted with telescopic forks.

They now come in all sizes and may have rebound-only or two-way damping, or no damping. In truth, there is never a total lack of damping, as the friction generated between the moving parts of the forks themselves provides some, but this is best kept to a minimum. The designers of modern machines go to some lengths to do this by reducing the stiction, or

force needed to start the parts moving, as this is invariably higher than the friction once they are on the move. By using modern materials and coatings, these forces can be minimized, but the older fork does suffer from this problem.

Telescopic forks comprise a pair of legs to which the wheel is fixed and a pair of stanchions, or tubes, which are held in the top and lower yokes. It is common for the legs to slide inside the tubes on cheap mopeds or lightweights, but outside them for most other machines. The springs may be internal or external, the former being more usual now, while the damping mechanism is fitted inside the fork legs in general, but can be an external unit.

The design can vary a good deal, but the essentials are the pairs of legs and tubes, the yokes, the springs and the damping mechanism. There are detail fixtures involved and a seal to retain the oil in each leg assembly. The legs may be steel or alloy, but the tubes are invariably steel and may be hard chromed. Usually the steering column will be incorporated into the lower yoke, but it can be in the upper one or it may be a separate part. The springs are usually steel and may be compound wound to give a variable rate, but air or rubber may be used for a similar effect. The damping is now always hydraulic, but has been by friction in the past.

The fork legs are braced to some degree by the mudguard fittings, but this aspect may be improved upon by the factory, or the owner, by the addition of a fork brace. These are

BELOW **First production model with hydraulically-damped telescopic forks was the BMW R12; this is a military version**

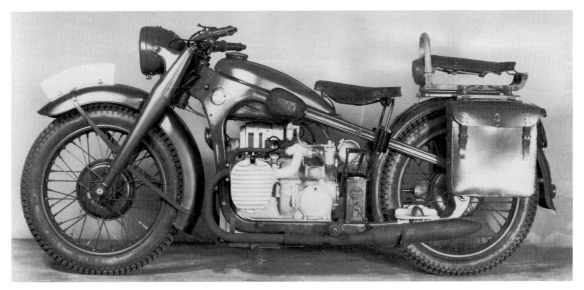

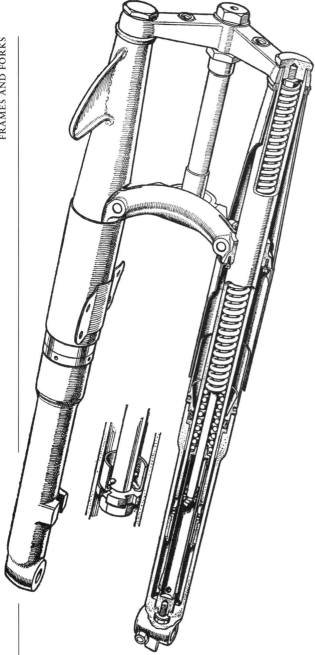

Norton Roadholder forks with hydraulic damping

items, as before, to leave the bare forks ready for attention. These may include shrouds or covers that conceal the tubes and may extend down to the legs to provide protection. The same result may be achieved with gaiters, although later forks often dispensed with anything to produce a 'slimline' look. The usual result was for flying stones to damage the tube's surface, which would then tear into the leg seal, allowing the oil to leak out.

Once the bars, wheel and mudguard are out of the way, it will be relatively easy to remove each leg assembly, as most are held by clamp bolts in each yoke. Simply slacken the bolt and the leg will come away, but first note how it fits in relation to the clamp, as this governs the ride height. If it does not align with the top of the yoke, take a measurement and write the figure down for use on assembly.

On older machines, the leg assembly is often held by a clamp in the lower yoke and a taper in the top one, being pulled up into the taper by a top nut. There is usually a tool for releasing the leg, which takes the place of the nut and can be given a smart blow with a mallet. The same tool may also be used to pull the stanchion up into place on assembly, as this can be an awkward job if it has to pass through a shroud.

If no tool is available, slacken the top nut a turn or two, place a piece of wood on it and use the mallet on this. As the leg assembly drops down, the nut can be removed, followed by the leg. This will release the shroud, which usually doubles as a headlamp support. Otherwise, remove any gaiter or external fork spring, plus anything clamped to the tube between the yokes, such as clip-on handlebars.

The fork yokes can then be dismantled and the head races attended to in the same manner as those for the girder fork. The yokes have a different form, but much of the work is the same, including the need to check alignment. If the machine has been in a crash, or had a heavy knock, there is a good chance that the forks will be bent and the yokes distorted.

Some checks may be better made with the yokes and stanchions assembled, but in all cases, any errors need to be corrected. In most, the forks should lay parallel to the steering column, but this is not always so, as some makers introduced a steering effect by slightly inclining one in relation to the other. Find out the figures and check the parts precisely, for a degree of

much more common as standard on modern machines, but many will benefit from the addition of one. They clamp on to the fork leg and are designed to provide the maximum bracing, while accommodating any tolerance between the legs.

Telescopic fork repair

As with the girders, the first step is dismantling, which is best begun by removing the external

BMW forks of 1975 with long travel, offset wheel spindle and exposed stanchions

error at the fork top can become quite noticeable down at the tyre's contact patch on the ground. The yokes must also be checked for any other signs of damage, distorted holes or poor threads. Anything found must be dealt with, and special attention should be paid to clamping lugs, for some are known to be liable to crack and then break off if over-tightened.

Next, the leg assemblies can be dealt with in turn, and preferably without mixing their parts. Each should be dismantled, using your manual to indicate the procedure. One possible trouble spot is removal of the seal holder, if this is part of a plated tube without a spanner hold, and a strap wrench, as mentioned earlier, may be the answer. Another problem can be the removal of any circlip holding the oil seal

in place and, for this, a suitable implement may have to be devised. Yet another concerns the damping assembly, which is often held in place by a single bolt inserted from below into the base of the fork leg. Such bolts are usually fitted using a Loctite compound and, even when slackened, may refuse to unscrew but, instead, simply rotate the internal mechanism. To overcome this, it will be necessary to hold the internal part, which can call for some ingenuity with nuts, bolts, tubular spanners and the like.

Once the leg assembly is apart, the details can be checked over and repaired, or replaced, as required. The stanchions are likely to need attention and may be worn, rusted, pitted or bent. The first three problems can be dealt with by hard chroming the part and then grinding it to size, but this expensive method should only be needed where new parts are not available. It is possible to fill pits with an epoxy resin, which can be smoothed down when hard, but this will only deal with minor damage.

The most common trouble with the tubes is that they will be bent, and they can be checked for this by rolling them on a flat surface or one on another. It is feasible to straighten a bent tube by using a hydraulic press, but this only works with minor bends and calls for skilled judgement as to how hard and far to push. With skill, the part can be restored, but if the metal has been stretched too far, there is no point in attempting the repair.

The fork leg may run directly on the stanchion in some cases, but in others, there will be bushes. The usual practice is to fit one on the lower end of the stanchion to work on the inside of the leg, while the second is fixed in the top of the leg, under the seal, and works on the stanchion. If worn, they will need replacement, which is usually easy for the upper bush, but may be less so with the lower one.

Wear on the stanchion may be dealt with by hard chroming, but a worn leg is less easy to cope with, other than by replacing it. With precision machinery, it is possible to bore out the leg to allow the fitment of a sleeve or the use of an oversize bush, but this must not be attempted lightly. The constraints are the need for the bore to be closely controlled, and the leg strength must not be materially reduced.

The oil seal should be replaced for convenience while the fork is apart, and any other seals or gaskets should also be checked and replaced if not completely fit for further duty. The studs and threads need to be checked over in the same manner as the yokes, with thread inserts being used to restore damage where needed. Pay particular attention to the wheel fixing and the brake anchor, as both areas are highly stressed. Where the wheel spindle is held by a clamp, make sure that this has not cracked, as it is a danger area on some models.

The fork springs should be checked for their free length and replaced if tired. Where this is not possible, it may be feasible to add packing to maintain the ride height, although this will reduce the fork travel and increase its rate a little. Make sure that it does not introduce a mechanical stop in place of a hydraulic one,

as this would greatly increase the loads on the fork parts.

The detail parts of the damping system all need to be checked over for condition and their ability to work freely and correctly. Springs and circlips may benefit from replacement, while it can be worth inspecting the damping oil holes and controls in case a previous owner has modified them. If this has happened, a reversion to standard is generally advisable, unless you are sure that the alterations are an improvement and really do work correctly.

The external shrouds, where used, also need attention, as they must fit quite accurately, even when holding the headlamp. Some are made in two parts, one being mounted between the yokes, often in rubber rings, and the other below the lower yoke. This last may be held in place by screws or the external fork spring, but it must run clear of the fork leg and any seal holder or extension to this, as must the one-piece shroud. If it does not, the parts will clash and wear as soon as the machine is used.

Where gaiters have been fitted in place of lower shrouds, they must be in good order without any tears or splits. They may be moulded to fit to the parts, or held in place by clamps, which must also be checked over. Some owners add gaiters to protect their fork stanchions from pitting and to give the oil seals an easier time. These are well worth retaining, but do check that they can do the job, will accommodate the full fork movement and are securely fixed in place. Gaiters usually have small holes in them to let air in and out, and these must be clear, but not mistaken for flaws in the parts.

Fork assembly is generally the reverse of dismantling and should give few problems. The head races should not be fully adjusted until the fork legs are in place to align the yokes, and it may be desirable to check on the alignment of the fork and the wheel spindle before proceeding too far.

Each fork leg can be assembled on the bench and then mounted in the yokes. Modern types with clamps will be no trouble, but the older ones with shrouds can pose a problem. This is the need to thread the stanchion up through the lower yoke and the shroud, into the top yoke taper, while keeping the leg fully extended.

A threaded bar that screws into the top of the stanchion will help, as this can be used to pull the part up, and it may then be held, temporarily, by tightening the lower yoke clamp. Then remove the tool, fit the top nut, undo the lower clamp and, finally, tighten the top nut. In the absence of the correct tool, it is possible to do the job using a broom handle, or a similar piece of wood, but this does carry the risk of debris dropping into the interior of the fork leg.

Do not finally tighten the lower clamp until the head races have been adjusted, as the yokes need to be able to move relative to each other. It may even be worth leaving this until the wheel is in place and the forks checked for their free movement, but this is not normally necessary. Such action is more usual when fitting the front wheel into the forks and, commonly, the clamp at the bottom of the fork leg should be left slack until the forks have been worked a couple of times to set the parts in alignment so that the forks do not bind.

The forks will need to be partially filled with oil to provide both damping and lubrication. It is well worth taking the trouble to make sure that both legs have the same amount of oil in them, and this may be by capacity or a direct oil level measurement. The first is simply a matter of pouring in the correct amount of the appropriate oil without allowing any to escape during the process. Some forks are more difficult to fill than others, so take your time if you have a pair like this. Air bubbles are the usual problem, so slow and steady pouring is the answer.

The oil quantity should be given in the manual and is best kept to, unless you have tried and proved otherwise. Variations would be fairly small. The oil is generally thin, and older machines often used SAE 20 monograde but, in time, this was replaced more and more by a specialized fork oil. This will be fine for most machines and owners, for it is only the competition rider who may need to fine-tune the suspension with changes to the damping oil. However, if your machine does suffer from inadequate or excessive damping, a change to thicker or thinner oil might be worth contemplating.

Many modern machine manuals may quote an oil quantity for each fork leg, but this is simply a convenience and an approximation. In use, both legs must be filled with oil to the same level, so this is the criterion and a procedure will be set out for checking this. Usually, it calls for the wheel to be off the ground and the fork fully extended, at which point the distance from the top yoke to the oil level can be checked with a rod to a dimension.

Telescopic fork variations

The notes above apply in general to the classic BSA, Norton and Triumph, together with the modern Honda and Kawasaki. Lightweights are generally the same, but simpler, without damping in many cases and rather crudely constructed with regard to bushes and oil or grease seals.

Suzuki fork leg and brake caliper with anti-dive attachment

This leaves a number of telescopic-type forks that fall outside these general patterns. Most need much the same attention to similar parts, but have their own idiosyncrasies and particular points to note.

One such was the Dowty Oleomatic fork, which was used in the late 1940s period by Panther, Scott and Velocette. This design dispensed with springs altogether. Instead, the suspension medium was air, which was compressed as the forks rose to give an excellent rising rate and, in theory, an effective non-metallic bump stop. In practice, the technology, which was based on Dowty's aircraft work, did not transfer too well to the motorcycle industry with its demands for larger quantities and much lower prices.

The Oleomatic fork was fine as long as the seals were in perfect order, but this was neither easy to arrange nor simple to maintain. Once a leak developed, the fork would collapse, and repair was somewhat complicated. Information on this and fork servicing can be found in *Velocette* by R. W. Burgess, published by C. A. Pearson and now out of print, but copies can be found at autojumbles.

The idea of using air as a springing medium has not been forgotten, but has been revived on many modern machines, where it assists the main spring. This reduces the pressures on it and ensures that a leak will not mean a fork collapse. Repair and restoration follows normal practice, with a special check on all the seals.

It is quite easy to add air assistance to modern forks by changing the top nuts for ones with air valves. If possible, the legs should be linked, as this makes it much easier to set the pressure, but this job should never be done with a normal air-line, as the pressure delivered would blow out the oil seals. Instead, a small handpump should be used with a special low-pressure gauge for the accuracy required. Make sure the pressure in each leg is the same if they are not connected, although this can be tedious to get right.

Modern forks may also have an anti-dive arrangement built into the damping circuit so that when the brakes are applied, the action stiffens up. There can also be adjustments for both the spring rate and damping, neither being a modern idea, although the early forms were often crude and the damping largely ineffective.

The ultimate development along this road is, no doubt, the competition fork, which has a massive range of adjustments to enable the rider to set up the machine to suit various circuits. For the road rider, sophistication comes in other forms, among them air-assisted forks and rear suspension with an on-board pump and controls to enable the settings to be varied on the road.

Rubber is a suspension medium usually associated with leading-link or girder forks, but it has also been used with telescopics. Dunlop produced a lightweight fork using this medium for a while, but better known is the Hagon type, which was built for grass-track racing and used rubber bands hooked onto pins. These are cheap, light and easy to change, so are excellent for their job.

One feature no longer found on modern forks is any means of adjusting the trail for sidecar use. On girder forks, this was done by changing a pair of links, and it is equally easy with the leading-link type described below. In fact, the modern answer is usually to fit such forks, as they are much more capable of coping with the side loads.

A few firms did allow for the sidecar man, and both Panther and Velocette contrived this by using a fork with the wheel spindle offset a little from the leg centre-line. Thus, by reversing the legs, the wheel spindle could be given an alternative position. Careful detail design gave the two desired trail dimensions and enabled all the parts to fit in either situation.

Royal Enfield and Norton tackled the problem in a different way by offering special sidecar forks. The former achieved their aim, initially, by offering alternative fork yokes, but from 1954 this was no longer feasible because of the casquette fitted to carry the headlamp. From then on, their solution was to extend the lower lugs of the fork legs to move the wheel spindle forward and, thus, reduce the trail. Norton adopted the first Enfield solution of alternative yokes from 1959, after Eric Oliver had demonstrated that the featherbed frame was up to sidecar work by racing a standard one in the TT.

The Scott telescopic fork has already been mentioned, and in its early form it had a centre spring above the wheel with a sliding tube on each side to link the parts. Later versions had the appearance of a girder fork, with this supporting the slide tube in which the lower leg

ABOVE LEFT **Moto Guzzi telescopics, which have an adjustable roller in place of a bottom bush**

LEFT **Royal Enfield fork end, which could be replaced by one with more offset for reduced sidecar trail**

moved. In either case, the result was true telescopic motion. Repair and renovation would be by a combination of the techniques used to restore both girder and telescopic forks.

The strange OEC system was also a telescopic fork in action, despite the odd arrangement for steering. As far as wheel movement was concerned, it followed a straight line along the head-angle axis and, thus, was telescopic, and an early example, too.

This was not so with the early Wooler plunger design, which had a small plunger housing on each side of the wheel spindle. This housing was supported by tubes running up to the lower fork yoke which, alone, took all the loads, as no top yoke was used. The layout had the plungers set vertically, so their movement

was in this direction, rather than along the steering axis. The post-war model differed in that there were two plunger housings on each side, the lower yoke was much more substantial, and the housings lay back at the headstock axis.

Leading-link forks

This is one of the oldest fork designs, and in the early days of motorcycling was offered as a bolt-on extra for machines with rigid forks. The type comes in many forms, but all are characterized by the fork pivot being positioned behind the wheel spindle. If the two are close together and the link short, they are referred to as leading-links. If the links are

long, with the pivot near to, or behind, the wheel and the links connected as one, they are commonly referred to as Earles forks, after Ernie Earles, who was much involved with the type in post-war years.

Regardless of this, they all act in the same way, only the radius of action varying. The manner in which the suspension medium is attached to the links, what that medium is, and how it is damped, are other matters, with a host of alternatives in existence. The actual fork action is also affected by the relative heights of the spindle and pivot at the static load position, and any attempt to alter this should be avoided, unless you are able to check that the change will not make the machine dangerous to ride.

The reaction of leading-link suspension under heavy braking will depend on how the backplate is anchored. If directly to the fork leg, this can cause the front end to rise if the reaction load exceeds the wheel load, which is usually the case. The effect can be disconcerting, as the forks will extend to full stretch so that they have no effective movement to cope with any bumps or ripples.

To overcome this, the brake backplate was anchored to the fixed part of the fork by a strut. To accommodate the wheel movement, it is necessary for both ends of the strut and the backplate to be free to pivot, and there must

ABOVE **Royal Enfield racing leading-links, which rely on the spindle clamp to hold the wheel upright**

ABOVE LEFT **Early Wooler with strange plunger units for front suspension. Post-war they did at least lay back at the fork angle**

be no play at the pivot points. By suitable arrangement of the strut length and pivot positions, this design can dip under braking or offer a designed degree of anti-dive. Remember that the loads involved are high, so your repair and restoration work must take account of this.

Leading-link repairs

The main fork member may be tubular or pressed-steel, so the techniques used to restore it need to be tailored accordingly. In either case, the head races will need the same attention as always, while alignment of them to the fork pivot is the major factor in straight-line steering.

The remainder of the work involved with this fork type concerns the fork legs or struts and the various bushes and bearings. The first will need inspection for damage of any kind and the second the same, replacement being the usual remedy. The pivot bearings may be taper-rollers, which will need careful cleaning, assembly and adjustment, but are more usually plain bushes.

The suspension medium may be attached directly to the links or be connected via some form of strut, which must be without slack in the joints. Compression coil springs are the most usual medium, but tension springs have been used, as have leaf springs, torsion bars and rubber. The first type are normally incorporated with dampers in the same form as common rear suspension units, and these are discussed in more detail in Chapter 7. In other cases, the damper may be separate from the suspension medium.

One of the most useful features of the leading-link fork is the ease with which the spring rate may be adjusted to suit varying loads. This may arise when a sidecar is fitted, and this type of fork is especially good at coping with the side loads involved. In addition, it is easy for a means of altering the trail to be included in the design, so this is often done.

The message that must be remembered from all these helpful details is to check just what the assembly is set up for. Make sure that spring units match from one side to the other, and that the fork trail is correct for your use.

Leading-link types

There is certainly nothing new about this type, for quite a number of early Edwardian models had leading-links since they could be easily added to rigid forks. In many cases, the short links were joined by a hoop over the wheel, the suspension spring being mounted above this and linked to either or both fork yokes.

Panther, Chater-Lea, Harley-Davidson and NSU are some who went along this route, and it was the American H-D design that later went on to many Brough Superior models. In time, Brough took to making them himself, as the Castle fork, but the layout remained little altered, with long springs concealed in tubes. Harley-Davidson continued with the type into the post-war era before switching to telescopics in the late 1940s, but the company did revert to the type for one model in 1988.

The early Bat machines had short leading-link front forks, but differed from others in that the links comprised a single tube that was bent to run round behind the wheel. Thus, they anticipated the Earles type in this feature by some 40 years or so, but their suspension medium

ABOVE **Very early add-on leading-link forks with twin tension springs on each side**

TOP **Bat leading-link joined by loop round wheel and supported by tension springs**

was by tension springs. These ran between the back of each main fork leg and the link behind its pivot point, so they were extended as the wheel rose. Many years later, the Motobecane scooter used a similar arrangement, but with rubber bands as the suspension.

A quarter-elliptic leaf spring may act as the suspension medium in this type of fork, being

ABOVE Douglas Radiadraulic forks with floating backplates, as used on the post-war models

BELOW DKR scooter with leading-link front forks typical of the machine type

clamped under the bottom yoke with its forward end linked by a strut to the wheel spindle area. This form of spring has some in-built damping, thanks to the friction between the spring leaves, but has limited movement and an untidy appearance.

The first post-war Douglas twins were designed with torsion bar front suspension. In truth, a coil spring is stressed in torsion when compressed, so the bar was simply the same technology applied in a different manner. It ran the full length of each main fork tube, being secured at the top and connected by a short strut to the leading-link at the bottom. A flat blade attached to the lower bar end was submerged in oil and fitted with a flap valve to provide the damping.

In production, this fork was replaced by the Radiadraulic design, which was still of the leading-link type, but had a long coil spring in each leg. This allowed more wheel movement and a much better damping arrangement, while the brake backplate was restrained by a floating strut.

Most post-war designs went along this route, the suspension units incorporating hydraulic damping and controlling short leading-links. Again, the layout was not new and had appeared on Edwardian NSU models, but a number of lightweights adopted it and often contrived to conceal the suspension units within the main fork, especially where this was constructed from pressings.

Honda used this type on many of their early models, and continued with it for their step-through range, as did other oriental firms. Few used the type for road racing, except for sidecars where the type is the normal equipment, but Moto Guzzi did for some time with considerable success. In part, this was due to using a large, hollow wheel spindle to help hold the links parallel to each other. NSU followed suit with their very successful works racers of 1953–4 and the Sportmax model used for racing and normal road work, while MV Agusta had an involvement with Earles forks in the early 1950s. This led to their use on a number of the company's road racing machines, including the works 500–4, which came about while Les Graham was sorting out that machine's handling.

The early Greeves machines used leading-link forks with rubber-in-torsion units acting as the suspension medium. These had inbuilt

Panther with leading-link forks, as well as engine acting as frame downtube

friction dampers, and the links were joined by a tube behind the wheel to provide a strong, rigid fork. In time, the rubber units and friction dampers were replaced by Girling spring and hydraulic dampers housed in the main fork tubes and, later still, by a revised design with external units, but the type remained as it was.

BMW was another firm to use leading-link forks for a while and fitted the Earles type from 1955 to 1969. Naturally, being BMW, they did the job properly and used taper-rollers for the fork pivot, but found, as had others, that the

ABOVE **Early Greeves front suspension with rubber in torsion for control and built-in friction dampers at pivot points**

ABOVE LEFT **Honda leading-link forks from a 125 of the 1960s with pressed-steel fork member and floating brake backplate**

LEFT **Adler front forks of 1954 with leading-links and floating torque arm**

extra weight swivelling about the headstock could introduce handling problems. Ariel went along the same road in 1953, but stopped short of production due, in part, to technical problems with weaving, rapid head race wear and poorer braking. Douglas used the Earles layout for their Dragonfly model but, in the main, the links, whether short or long, were only found on lightweights, scooters and mopeds after that.

Trailing-link forks

With this type, the fork pivot lies ahead of the wheel spindle, which would seem to offer distinct advantages in allowing the wheel to trail over road irregularities. This is so, but the extra weight of the link supports, placed well ahead of the headstock axis, introduces an even greater handling problem than with the leading-link type.

In addition, appearance is often poor, unless the links are kept short, and the normal nosedive effect when braking will be compounded if the backplate is anchored directly to the link arm. This occurs on some scooters, where its effect is acceptable, but in most cases, the type looks ungainly.

The early Indian models had trailing-links with a quarter-elliptic spring anchored under the bottom yoke as the suspension medium. A strut linked the wheel to the front end of the spring and, at first, ran from the spindle to push the spring up as the wheel rose. Later, the link was extended ahead of its pivot and the strut connected there, so the spring was pulled down as the wheel went up. The designs were used for many years, including 1941 on the in-line four.

The same design appeared on the first BMW

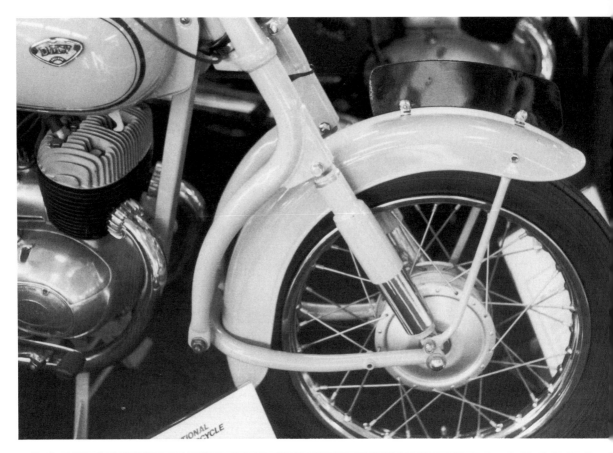

ABOVE Trailing-link forks, as used by BMW for may years until they turned to telescopics and here with pressed-steel blades to match the frame

ABOVE LEFT DMW with Earles-type, long leading-link forks with the arms joined behind the wheel

LEFT Honda C90 scooterette with short leading-links that provide adequate suspension

flat-twin of 1923, and was used by them until 1938, although they had begun the change to telescopics a little earlier. In most cases, a simple curved tube supported the link on each side, but machines with pressed-steel frames used the same construction technique for their fork blades.

The original Greeves had a trailing-link fork, but with a loop connecting the links ahead of the front wheel. With this, plus a trailing brake anchor strut, the appearance was odd, and in production leading-links were used. Even the works Norton road racer was tried with the trailing-link design at a couple

of meetings in 1953, but it was not proceeded with.

Lambretta and Vespa both used trailing-link suspension for their very popular scooters and, while these may have been technically inefficient, there was no doubt as to their dominance of the market. With either machine, heavy braking does force the suspension right down, but it proved adequate for its job.

One of the best known post-war motorcycle applications of the trailing-link fork was on the Ariel Leader, and Arrow models derived from it. These machines had a pressed-steel main fork with forged alloy links and enclosed spring-and-damper units. The brake backplate was anchored by a link to the main fork, and the design worked well.

Trailing-link forks can be repaired and restored in the same manner as leading-link versions, making the same checks for damage, cracks, splits, poor threads and worn bearings. The head races need attention as usual, and alignment is as important as always. The suspension medium may be spring-and-damper units, as used elsewhere, or otherwise, but the techniques remain the same.

Other fork types

These comprise the hub-centre types, from which have developed some interesting wishbone designs, aimed at either allowing a low seating position on the machine or simply overcoming some of the inherent faults in the telescopic fork design. They are often much eulogized by the 'feet forward' enthusiasts as part of their call to move on from bicycle technology and layout.

The idea is not new, as the best known early example was the Ner-a-Car of the 1920s, which had a single wishbone holding a fixed kingpin on which the wheel pivoted. Side arms carried the springs, and the restricted suspension movement did not alter the kingpin angle too much.

In the post-war years, the Difazio design used a double wishbone layout, as did the Elf and Hossack. All involve a number of spherical bearings, and most tend to limit steering lock and have some difficulty in feeding braking loads back to the main frame.

Restoration of such systems is no different to others, despite the appearance, with inspection, repair and replacement in the usual manner. All bushes and bearings need to be in really good order to allow movement without play.

Steering damper

For many years, these were based on friction discs in the same form as used by many girder forks. They suffered the same problem of the initial stiction being higher than the moving friction and, eventually, were superseded by a hydraulic design. Some of these were drum-shaped, while others were telescopic, but all

LEFT **Ariel trailing-link forks, as used on their Leader and Arrow models, with the suspension units concealed under the pressings**

ABOVE LEFT **Lambretta with trailing-link forks, which dip greatly on braking, but work well enough on scooters**

ABOVE RIGHT **Hub-centre suspension and steering, as developed for the Ner-a-Car of the 1920s**

RIGHT **Elegant Foale front suspension of the 1980s, as used on the Project QL machine**

operated by forcing oil through a restriction.

The friction type needs to be dismantled and the details cleaned ready for inspection. Often, they will be heavily coated with grease from the lower head race, which does nothing for their efficiency. The Andre type, which puts the disc assembly above the headstock, avoids this, but normally involves a strap anchor on to the petrol tank.

The main damper rod thread must be in good order if it is to load the plates smoothly, and the knob itself is often threaded on to the rod and then cross-pinned. The rod should be straight, otherwise it will tilt the plates, which must be flat and smooth. The anchor plate must be fixed to the frame without play or any tendency to deflect the plates on either side of it and, thus, may fit over a pin.

The steering damper of a solo does not have to do a great deal of work, which is why its operation must be smooth. The friction discs must, therefore, be flat and of an even thickness to allow for this, but in sidecar use, the loads are higher. For this, it is essential that the friction surfaces are not contaminated with grease, otherwise the damper will be ineffective.

On assembly, especially with a solo, make sure the damper comes into action easily and

ABOVE **Hossack with wishbone front suspension derived from car type, and special rear as well**

ABOVE RIGHT **Steering damper knob with spring clip to hold its set position on a BSA Gold Star**

BELOW **Typical friction damper under lower race, so easily covered with grease**

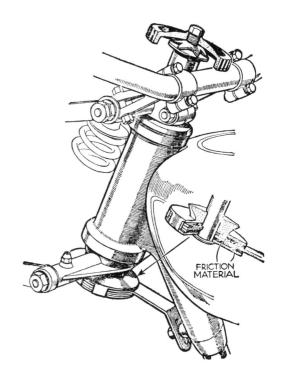

FRICTION MATERIAL

provides an even level of damping as the forks turn from lock to lock. Any variation could be hazardous in use and must be eradicated. It is most likely to be caused by bent parts or the action of bolting the anchor in place. Straightening and, sometimes, the addition of packing washers may cure the problem.

Some machines have a means of locking the damper knob in its set position, and this is usually by a form of spring clip. This, too, must be in order and strong enough to do its job without making adjustment of the setting too hard to alter.

Hydraulic steering dampers are often sealed assemblies, which limits repair or restoration to their fixings and general condition. Given suitable facilities, it may be feasible to strip and rebuild such parts, but they do not lend themselves to this. The telescopic type is often adjustable by means of a screw valve in the restrictor line, but for some BMW flat-twins, the same effect was obtained by varying the operating radius of the damper.

Safety note

It is imperative that all work on the front forks and all associated parts is carried out to the highest standards. Any structural failure is bound to be unpleasant, and this must be avoided by full inspection and checking of all parts.

Be especially careful of modifications away from standard, which could affect strength or steering geometry. For the same reasons, beware of fitting different forks or parts from other machines. All will be fine if carried out correctly, but a disaster if not!

CHAPTER 6
Rear suspension

For many years, very few machines had any rear suspension at all, the rider having to rely on the saddle and rear tyre for insulation from road shocks. While this was the norm until well after World War 2, there were always exceptions, and some forms of rear suspension were in use in Edwardian times.

Most of the early designs lacked rigidity, offered no damping of the movement and were flimsy in their construction, so acceptance was slow. Often, the suspension was associated with one of the interesting, forward-looking, advanced machines that so often failed to either reach production or maintain it for any length of time. ABC was one, but others, such as the Indian, did succeed, but more in their own country.

In Britain, firms kept to rigid frames for the period between the wars with a few notable exceptions. There was some drift to rear suspension towards the latter part of the 1930s, following Woods' two TT victories on rear-sprung Guzzis, which helped this trend. It was fostered by the racing successes of several firms in 1938–9, but then the war kept most riders on rigid frames for the duration.

After the war, maximum production was the priority, so technical development was restricted for some years. Then, rear suspension began to become more usual, but with a divergence of opinion between the plunger and pivoted-fork systems. The first was often so

Plunger rear suspension on a post-war BSA, and a type common to much of their range

Early pivoted-fork rear suspension with leaf spring and linkages to join the details together

easily added to an existing rigid frame that it was some while before firms moved to the, now universal, pivoted fork. Along the way, there had been one or two other systems, such as the Triumph sprung hub and Ariel link, but both gave a curved movement to the rear wheel, similar to the pivoted fork.

Plunger systems nearly always have coil springs as the suspension medium, with rare exceptions where rubber has been used. Pivoted-fork systems have used spring, air and rubber mediums, the first being the most usual and sometimes combined with the second. Early machines employed leaf springs, but coil springs in compression have been by far the most popular means, although there have been users of tension springs and torsion bars.

The feature that sets off one pivoted-fork system from another is the way in which the fork is connected to the suspension system. There are a great many possible methods with modern types offering much sophistication, but all remain pivoted forks. Other than today's complex rising-rate and floating-unit layouts, most have been tried in the past, a crude version of the modern monoshock appearing as early as 1904.

Therefore, it is important when dealing with pivoted-fork designs, to distinguish between the fork itself, the suspension medium and the connection between the two. The suspension unit and its damping are yet another story, which follows in Chapter 7.

Plunger systems

The heyday of this type came in the late 1940s, but it was nothing new, for examples were to

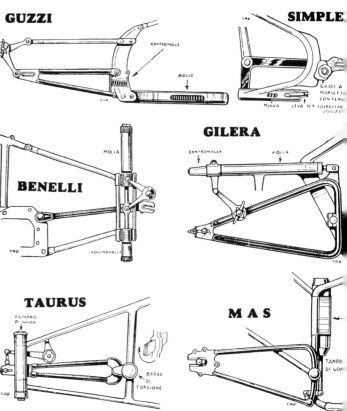

ABOVE A whole variety of rear suspension systems that were in production on Italian machines in the late 1930s

LEFT Excelsior lightweight rear suspension, which differed from most in that the plunger boxes moved with the wheel

be seen prior to World War I. Most follow the same lines, with a fixed pillar clamped between the frame supports, a bushed slider incorporating the wheel spindle lugs, and springs top and bottom, plus covers for these.

The design lacked damping in nearly all cases, although it could be added, usually externally, and what there was came from the friction of the system. This varied a good deal, as it depended on the tolerances and wear of the parts and on how well the width across the wheel hub matched the gap between the spindle lugs. If the same, then the wheel would not affect the plunger operation, but if there was a mismatch in either direction, the sliders would be forced against the pillars with increased friction.

The plungers had to rely on the wheel spindle to hold them in alignment and the wheel upright, so larger detail parts and a good fit in the lug slots became essential. A further snag with the system is that the chain tension varies, being slackest at the middle position, where it spends most of its time, simply to avoid being over-tight if the suspension should go to full travel. The pivoted fork is the reverse, the chain being at, or very near, correct adjustment normally and only becoming rather slack on extreme deflections of the suspension.

Plunger repairs

The first task is to dismantle each assembly, and a word of warning is necessary, as they are

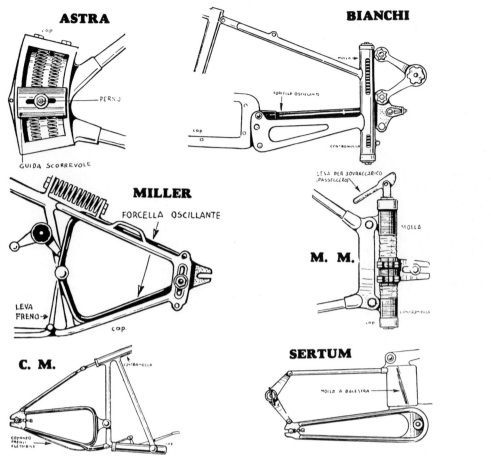

ASTRA

CAP
PERNO
GUIDA SCORREVOLE

BIANCHI

MOLLA
FORCELLA OSCILLANTE
CAP
CONTROMOLLA

MILLER

FORCELLA OSCILLANTE
LEVA FRENO
CAP.

LEVA PER SOVRACCARICO (PASSEGGERO)
MOLLA

M. M.

CONTROMOLLA
CAP

C. M.

CONTROMOLLA
COMANDO FRENI FLESSIBILE
CAP.

SERTUM

MOLLA A BALESTRA

under some degree of compression. In practice, it is usually feasible to cope with most light- and mediumweight machines without a compression tool, but only as long as you are aware of what can happen as the spring boxes are released.

Dismantling normally commences with the removal of the central pillar, which may be held in place by clamp bolts, end screws or a combination of both. With these removed, the pillar can come out, but check for any restriction, such as the tapered lower fixing of the Norton, that will dictate in which direction it must be removed. Also, check whether any bolt needs to come right out because it fits into a groove on the pillar or is simply a clamp.

The pillar may slide out easily or need some assistance, which can involve a long rod and a hammer. If the pillar is hollow with pressed-in end caps, this may unseat the caps, rather than move the pillar, and care may be needed

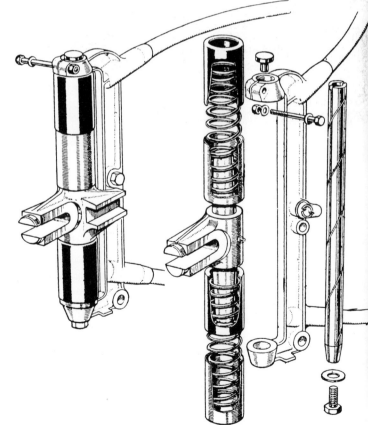

Norton plunger rear suspension, the spindle of which must come out from the top

ABOVE **Condor 1953 model with shaft drive and plunger rear suspension**

ABOVE RIGHT **Traditional pivoted-fork machine in the form of a 1961 Norton Manxman with American bars**

to avoid damage to any internal thread in the pillar end. For stubborn cases, this can be used with a suitable puller or slide hammer to extract the part.

As it comes out, be careful not to lean on the spring boxes, as this could cause them to fly out. While these are still secure in the frame, it is usually possible to get an idea as to whether you can compress the springs and ease the assembly out. If you can, then well and good, but make sure the frame cannot roll during the operation, otherwise the parts may slide out of your grasp.

Where the spring loads are too high for this, you will need a compressor, which is simply a long threaded rod with nuts, spacers and washers at each end. This is used by levering the spring box assembly out just enough to expose the central pillar hole and then fixing the threaded rod through this. Tighten the nuts enough to compress the springs, remove the assembly from the frame, unwind the nuts and the details will come apart.

All will need a thorough clean, for they will be heavily coated with old grease, long since solidified. Once clean, they can be examined and checked over for damage or wear. The pillar may be worn or corroded, depending on its earlier life, and in either case will need replac-

ing. The part is simple to make if no spares are to be had, but before going to these lengths, check whether one of the popular BSA pillars can be modified to suit, as they are more likely to be available.

The sliders are the next items to check over, and often each comprises a forged lug for the spindle with a separate slider tube, either pressed or clamped into the lug. The tube may run directly on the pillar or incorporate bushes, and replacement of one or the other is the usual answer to wear.

The slider usually carries a grease nipple for lubrication, and this must be in good order and not blocked. Also, check its hole and any others that carry grease to the working surfaces, including any grooves in bushes or on the pillars. Any other threads or holes also need to be checked and may exist to clamp the wheel spindle, be part of the brake anchor or involved with the chain adjustment.

The springs should be checked to see if they

have become shorter, as they do tire after many years, and any spring collars examined to ensure that they hold parts square and in-line. This may involve the spring shrouds, which are also prone to wear and corrosion. They need to slide over each other without removing the finish and, to do this, must sit correctly against the frame and spindle lugs. Replacements are available for common makes in standard or stainless steel, but check that they fit and perform as they should.

Assembly is the reverse of dismantling, with the same strictures regarding the fitting of the spring boxes into the frame. If in doubt, use a compression rod to be sure. Make sure the assembly is well greased, and do not neglect this aspect of maintenance, as regular attention will keep the parts in order for many miles.

Normally, there is no adjustment with a plunger system, but ensuring that the wheel is a nice fit between the spindle lugs is a good measure. Rarely, will there be any damping, unless a previous owner has added some, but there are always exceptions, and Levis made an attempt in 1939. Owner modifications tend to be either external, friction lever-arms or hydraulic cylinder types.

Pivoted fork

'As old as the industry, as modern as the hour', as Riley advertised its cars, and this was also applicable to pivoted-fork suspension, which was first seen in Edwardian days. It is now the standard system for just about all machines, and these really only differ in the way in which the fork is connected to its controlling spring and damper. The type is often referred to as swinging-arm suspension, but this term really only applies where a single member supports the rear wheel.

The most common arrangement for the suspension medium is as twin units, one on each side, between the fork ends and the frame. There are, of course, many others, the spring unit being mounted above or below the engine or the rear fork, in plunger boxes, within frame members, or as part of a modern complex linkage and not directly fixed to the frame at all. Most incorporate some means of connecting the fork and unit, which may be simple or involved.

All systems have at least one pivot, which is the one on which the fork or arm moves. There may be more, and the suspension units themselves usually have one at each end to accommodate a degree of movement and working tolerances.

The fork pivot is normally placed as close to the gearbox centre as possible to minimize the effect the wheel movement will have on chain tension. A short fork, in practice two short links, as used by OEC in the late 1930s, is much poorer in this respect. It also lacks rigidity, as the wheel spindle has the impossible task of holding the links parallel while providing a means of adjusting the chain tension.

Pivoted-fork dismantling

Most of the suspension should dismantle easily, with little need for pullers or special tools. Remember that while this is true for most conventional layouts, there are those where the springs are housed under load and, for these, it is necessary to take precautions to avoid accidents. Once the unit is out of the way, this will leave the main fork attached by its pivot to the frame, and this can introduce problems on some machines.

Many modern machines have the fork secured by a single, long bolt, removal of which is generally easy. In some cases, it may be tight,

due to corrosion, and need a press to assist it on its way, but rarely will it require cutting to allow the parts to separate. The same usually applies where the fork sits between frame members with a central tie-rod, or bolt. Again, removal is normally easy. This should also be the case for the fork itself, but not always, as it may be necessary to spread the frame a little to release the fork.

Far more of a problem is the type where the pivot spindle is pressed into a frame lug and the fork has a bush at the front of each leg to work on this. The legs will be joined by a cross-tube just behind the pivot and, thus, the only way to dismantle the assembly is to remove the spindle. This design is to be found on Triumph twins, AMC models and BSA Bantams, all of which are equally awkward to deal with. In some instances, the spindle ends are tapped and support plates are added to brace the assembly, but they seldom offer more than a token improvement. The design is inherently poor and offers no real support to stop the fork pivot twisting the frame.

Removing the spindle may call for a press

ABOVE **Well supported rear fork with frame member at each side for the pivot pin**

LEFT **A true swinging arm in light alloy for the Honda VFR750R, with a rather complex floating caliper linkage**

and, in most cases, the operation is difficult due to the need to support the whole frame at the same time. In addition, the press movement and working clearance must be large enough to accommodate the spindle length and the distance it has to move. Before operating the press, check for any locking screws or cotter pins, which may be present to secure the pivot, and remove or slacken them as required. AMC, alone, made the job easy by pressing the spindle into a bridge piece that was bolted to the frame, but only up to 1955.

This difficult job is often made worse by a lack of lubrication during the machine's life. Thus, the bushes and spindles may wear badly, and the latter can generate a wear ridge, which will stop the spindle from coming out. With access totally restricted until the parts have been dismantled, it is usually impractical to file this away, and applying extra pressure may cause the housing hole to open up.

The alternative to wear is seizure, which can be worse, as the spindle will have turned in its housing and the wear will have enlarged the hole. A press should manage the job, in this instance, but where it cannot, it can be helped by heating the parts. This often enables the press to do its job, but if all else fails, the only solution is to cut through the spindle.

The Norton Commando has a similar system, the spindle being held by a single bolt or two cotter pins. It should pull out, either by hand or with the help of an extractor bolt, but at least its housing is part of the rear engine plate assembly, which is separate from the main frame.

For some of their models, AMC avoided much of this trauma by making one fork leg separate from the spindle and remaining leg. It should be a close fit on the spindle and secured by a cotter pin, but once this has been removed, the parts should dismantle without further trouble. If the spindle has seized in its bearings, a press will be needed, but this is not usual.

Velocette took this type further on their singles, both fork legs being clamped on to a separate spindle. This pivoted in bushes in a frame lug, and these are prone to wear if not

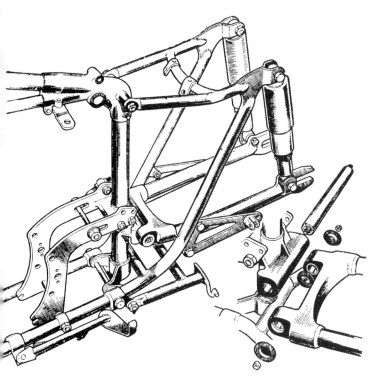

kept well lubricated. The spindle has three different diameters, that for the right leg being slightly larger than the bearing, and that for the left leg smaller. The right leg has a groove in the spindle hole to identify it, but this was hardly necessary as the left leg had extra lugs for the chainguard and rear brake.

Correct alignment of these types is essential, and the Velocette also requires a tool to press the legs fully on to the spindle, compress the oiling felts and remove all end-float. Mandrels will enable the parts to be set, and while sight lines may prove adequate, it is better to use a surface plate and measuring equipment.

The post-war Velocette range included the

LEFT Triumph twin pivoted fork of 1954 with awkward pressed-in pin and limited pivot housing support

BELOW Puch military model with twin-link rear suspension designed to give constant chain tension

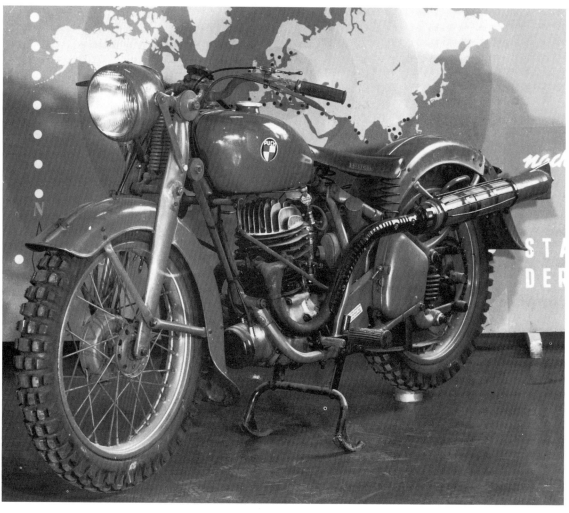

LE model with shaft drive and, like all with this feature, it could not have a pivot spindle running across the rear fork. This is because the shaft's universal joint is positioned at this point, so the spindle has to be in two sections, one on each side.

They mount to the frame to offer a fixed pin in bushes, or bearings, installed in the rear fork, and one, or both, may be adjustable to limit or set the side-play. Dismantling should prove no problem, but will involve uncoupling the drive shaft.

Pivoted-fork repair

The rear fork requires the same checks as the main frame for cracks, distortion or damage. The first should show up under inspection, the second can be checked with a surface plate and mandrels, while the last may be obvious or call for a close examination.

Any threads must be in good order, especially those involved with the suspension-unit attachment or rear brake anchorage. Include the chain adjusters in this, regardless of whether they are the usual screw type or an eccentric design at the pivot point.

The main items likely to need attention are the pivot bearings and the spindle. The former are normally a press fit into the fork and may be bushes, needle races, taper-rollers or bonded rubber. They may press out, but often need some part to be made to enable this to be done. A bar that fits across the bearing on its inside may do the job, or it could call for a special bearing extractor.

There is often a distance piece between the bearings, which may be an essential spacer or simply a means of keeping the grease where it is needed. In the former application, it must never be left out, otherwise the bearings will soon fail, while in the latter, its omission will allow you to fill the entire rear fork with unwanted grease.

The new bearings will press in, and bushes are likely to need reaming to size. Where this is the case, or where they have been made from bar anyway, it pays to check the spindle first. If this is no longer a good fit in the frame lug, where this applies, either an oversize spindle, along with suitable bushes, will be needed, or the frame lug will have to be renovated. This can be done by boring and fitting a sleeve, but accuracy and correct alignment are essential.

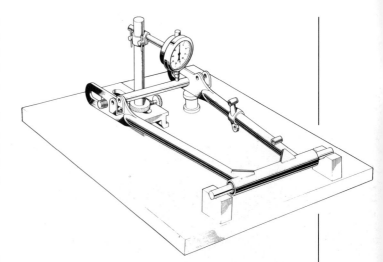

Checking alignment of rear fork with surface plate and dial gauge

The spindle will need renewal if worn or corroded and, together with the bushes, it may need oil or grease holes in various locations. These are essential to avoid further wear in the future, and all must be clean, free of blockages and supplied by nipples in good order. Do not forget any seals or felt oil retainers in the assembly.

Needle and taper-roller bearings will either be fine or worn out, few being between these conditions. If in good order, they will only need cleaning and fresh grease, but also check any oil seals in the assembly, replacing them if in any doubt as to their condition. Normally, they are best changed as a matter of convenience, while the parts are dismantled. Needle-rollers can indent into their inner race, so these are best changed if there is any sign of this, and always if the races are renewed. In the same way, all taper-roller bearings must be changed as an assembly and, ideally, in pairs.

Bonded rubber offers a bearing with no moving surfaces and good rigidity, so was popular on many machines. The rubber can degrade and come away from its surrounding tube, or be destroyed by fire, any of which will leave the outer tube in the housing. It can be pressed or pulled out if a suitable mandrel is made up, but often requires cutting out to dislodge it. New parts simply press in, but the load must be on the outer and any space between the inners taken up by a distance tube.

Rear suspension systems that do not have the basic twin spring-and-damper units to control them are likely to have more links and bear-

ings. This is as true for modern rising-rate designs as pre-war monoshock or under-engine arrangements, and all the additional parts need to be checked. Most, or all, of the work will be on the same lines, the parts needing to be dismantled, inspected, repaired, and rebushed, and threads checked.

Always remember that you are dealing with a system that may incorporate springs under load, so make sure that their energy is not suddenly released to injure you or anyone else. Also, remember that a failure of a structural part could cause an accident while riding, so these, in particular, need treating with care.

Pivoted-fork assembling

This should be simply a reversal of the dismantling process, with lubrication of the bearings as required. A press may be needed to install the pivot spindle, and shims may be called for in this area to restrict side-play.

Few designs will offer any major problems, but the manual will indicate if there are any and how to attend to them. Alignment of the fork legs, where separate, has already been mentioned, as has the setting of pivot bearings. These may require some preload, otherwise aim for free movement with no play.

ABOVE **Vincent monoshock rear suspension with their dualseat support links incorporating friction dampers**

RIGHT **Honda Pro-link shown assembled on a 1981 CR480R–B**

The rubber bush bearing has one point to note on assembly, and this is to hold the fork at its mid-travel position while the fixings are being tightened. This is to keep distortion of the rubber to a minimum and is easy enough to arrange, using a length of cord to hold the fork as needed.

Most pivot bearings require grease for lubrication, but some, such as AMC and the Norton Commando, demand oil. These machines have a sealed reservoir built into the rear fork housing, and this must be free of grease. If any is present, it is likely to block the oil holes to the bearings, which will then wear rapidly.

Pivoted-fork systems

The most common has twin spring-and-damper units, but there were many variants of this design before the modern rising-rate types arrived. The latter all use a system of links and bell-cranks or rocking arms to achieve a rising-rate of both spring and damper, which are combined in a single unit. This is not normally attached to the frame at all, but mounts between the rear fork and one of the links, so it moves as it is compressed and extended.

This is the one feature that distinguishes the modern system from the old, for in the past, at least one end of the spring would be anchored to the frame. As regards its position, this varied as much as on a modern chassis.

The monoshock, in crude form, dates from Edwardian times and has resurfaced at regular intervals over the years. In Britain, Bentley & Draper, New Imperial and Vincent-HRD designs appeared between the wars, while Italian forms appeared on CM and Miller, a German one on NSU, and a French version on the Clément. Years later, Yamaha revived the type with a much refined spring-and-damper unit.

The basic twin units have a little variation, in that they may be inclined, or moved forward to be attached to the fork nearer to its pivot,

or both. These moves originated from the scrambles or motocross world, where they allowed more movement, but at the expense of working the damper section much harder. Velocette used the inclination to alter the effective spring rate to suit solo or twin riders, and made this adjustable with a curved slot for the unit's top mounting. Most other firms incorporate the method of adjustment, if any, in the spring unit itself.

If the springs are mounted beneath the engine, some form of bell-crank linkage is needed to connect them to the fork. This can be arranged so that tension springs are used instead of the usual compression ones, or even both. Moto Guzzi and Simplex were two Italian firms to use this principle during the 1930s, while Gilera reversed it so that the springs were housed in tubes above, and parallel to, the fork legs.

Some makes combined a pivoted fork with plunger spring boxes, a suitable link being provided between the two, and examples of this design can be found on Benelli, Bianchi, DKW

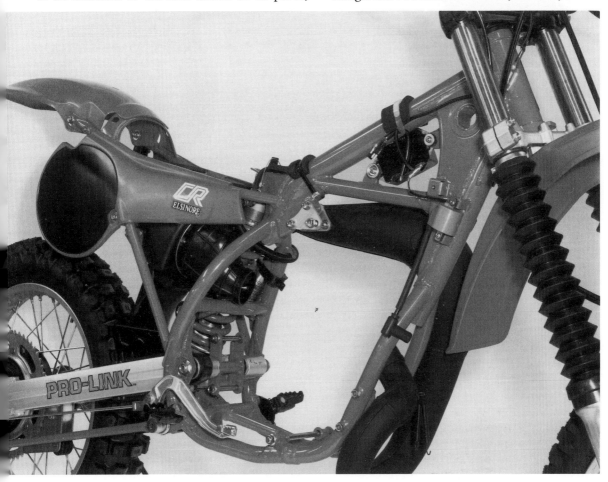

and OEC pre-war, and the Royal Enfield Ensign post-war. Often, they could be mistaken for plunger systems, but a closer examination will show the links and their bushes and bearings.

Post-war, there were variations on the theme from Greeves and Tandon, both of whom used rubber for the suspension at first. Greeves used the same rubber units in torsion as at the front, and these were mounted in the top corners of the subframe. Links on each side were connected to the fork ends, and the lever lengths were adjusted to provide the required spring rate. The Tandon differed in having its rubber mounted close to the fork pivot and compressed to give the suspension.

The torsion bar was also used for rear suspension, and its best known motorcycle application is on the post-war Douglas twin. There were two torsion bars, which ran the length of the lower frame tubes, each with an anchor at the front and a link at the rear running up to the fork. There was no damping, although it would have been easy to add, but the splines on the ends of the torsion bar made it easy to adjust the ride height to suit the carriage of heavier loads. Hardly a rider alteration, but handy to the firm during development work.

Torsion-bar rear suspension was used by the early D and LD model Lambretta scooters, the bar being housed in the frame just ahead of the rear wheel. With these models, the complete engine, gearbox and transmission was one assembly, which included the arm carrying the rear wheel. The whole pivoted about a point beneath the crankcase, the torsion bar being

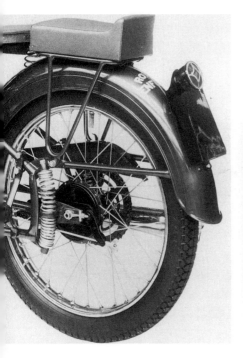

ABOVE **Royal Enfield with plunger springs linked to pivoted fork by screwing into lug on fork**

ABOVE LEFT **Velocette single with slotted top rear unit mountings for adjustment of suspension rate**

ABOVE RIGHT **Greeves rear suspension with links up to rubber torsion units incorporating friction dampers**

LEFT **Gilera with pivoted rear fork controlled by spring units above it with bell-crank linkage**

attached by lever and link to the engine, and a separate hydraulic damper was fitted between the frame and the rear end of the arm. It worked well, but called for some special tools to wind up the bar on assembly.

Leaf springs have been used in the past to control pivoted-fork suspension, and these have usually been mounted above the rear fork from the saddle mountings. The springs extended to the rear in quarter-elliptic form and were linked to the fork on each side, often being joined over the wheel to help keep it upright. Such designs were used by ABC, Douglas and Indian, while other firms arranged the spring differently so that it acted in a monoshock form. Panther produced a variation for its projected 1940 range, the rear fork also being formed from two leaf springs. These were coupled by vertical links to another higher, set of springs, and it was the links that carried the wheel spindle. Due to the war and technical problems, the system never went into production.

Alternative rear suspension

These are systems that do not fall readily into the plunger or pivoted-fork categories, although they usually control the wheel so that it moves in an appropriate arc about the gearbox sprocket for constant chain tension.

An early type is the semi-elliptic leaf spring, as used by Megola and Coventry Eagle between the wars. It is not a very suitable system for motorcycles due to the need for a substantial mounting at the rear of the machine, but renovation follows the same lines as for other leaf springs.

More common are the Ariel link and Triumph sprung hub, both of which sought to move the wheel in a true arc about the sprocket, albeit over a restricted distance. The Ariel design first appeared in 1939, as an option for most of the range, and was still in use on the Square Four 20 years later.

The Ariel linkage was designed by Frank Anstey and used plungers with load and rebound springs on each side. The slider between them did not carry the wheel spindle as usual, but a cross-pin that connected it to

ABOVE Douglas rear fork with link on each side to torsion bar running length of frame lower tube

BELOW The Ariel plunger and link rear suspension system used to give constant chain tension at the cost of too many bushes

a stirrup This was slotted at the rear for the wheel spindle and, at the front, linked to the frame tube by short plates. As the wheel rose and fell, the stirrup moved with it and tilted under the control of the links so that the spindle described the desired arc.

For the sake of constant chain tension, the design included far too many small bearings, and once these wore, the wheel spindle could no longer hold the wheel upright. Greasing is necessary at very regular intervals to avoid this problem developing, but even when new, the system was weak on wheel support and without any damping, other than from friction.

The Triumph sprung hub was designed in 1938, but not offered until 1947, when it became an option, after which it remained available up to 1954. The large, full-width hub enclosed the entire spring and slider assembly, which was why the movement was limited to 2 in. and had no damping. The internal slider and the casting bolted around it were curved to give the movement an arc form, and within the casting sat the springs under considerable stress.

Triumph sprung hub, which fits the post-war rigid frame. Its interior must not be dismantled without the correct tools

The castings have a 'do not disturb' message cast into the metal, and with good reason. It is very dangerous to attempt to dismantle the spring box without the correct special tool, and this must not be attempted under any circumstances. People have been badly hurt ignoring this warning, and the springs have been known to punch holes in workshop roofs where owners have done this.

The casting assembly carries the two bearings on which the hub revolves, and this is the main difference between the Mark I and II types. The former has loose ball bearings adjusted with shims, while the latter has large bore ball races. The full procedure for servicing these hubs is set out in the appropriate manuals, but it must again be emphasized that the casting assembly must not be disturbed without the correct tools.

CHAPTER 7
Suspension units

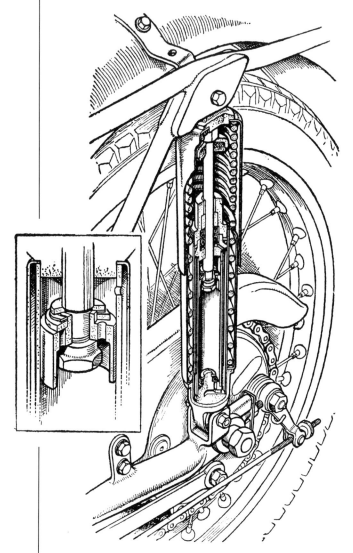

Norton rear suspension unit, as used by the first 88 twins in 1952

These control the movement of the wheels and usually combine both spring and damping into one telescopic unit. They may be found on front or rear wheels and, on occasion, the two functions may be separated, or damping may not be provided at all. In the early days, it was usual for damping to be by friction and separate from the springs, but it was convenient to combine the two once hydraulic damping became normal.

The various alternatives to compression coil springs have already been mentioned and include tension, torsion, leaf and air, each of which has been used as a suspension medium. Virtually all modern machines use compression coil springs, but a number also include air within the unit to assist in varying the spring rate.

Air, alone, was used in the Dowty rear unit fitted to the Mk VIII KTT Velocette racing machines, but this produced problems of maintaining the pressure, sealing, and the effects of the air heating up as the unit worked. In modern units, gas under pressure is commonly employed to assist the damper in its operation.

The suspension units often have some means of increasing their spring rate to cater for the addition of a passenger or heavy loads. Most commonly, this is by a cam ring, which increases the spring preload, but on their post-war models Velocette varied the working angle of the unit to achieve the same result. With air units, this can be done by raising the internal pressure.

Damping rates are commonly fixed, but both the original friction type and the more modern hydraulic ones may be varied sometimes while riding. Competition units often offer many choices of setting to allow the rider to select the optimum for the circuit, its condition and any other factors.

For a while, in the 1980s, many sports models were given a good range of adjustments, but this practice did not last for long. Few riders actually made any real use of them, and their presence made it possible for some to ignore the manual and set their machines up in a less than safe way.

Girder fork dampers

It is quite feasible to use hydraulic damping with this fork type, as demonstrated by Vincent with their Girdraulic type, but friction discs were the norm. These were usually incorporated on one of the fork spindles, the lower front one being popular, but by no means standard.

The disc assembly was similar to a steering damper, and its effect could be adjusted with a knob or wing-nut. It is important that the thread and detail parts do not interfere with the action and adjustment of the girders themselves, so they must be removed or slackened off while the forks are set up.

The detail parts need cleaning and inspecting for wear and damage, replacement being normal for the discs if worn. Check the spindle and knob or wing-nut threads for wear, the working disc faces for damage and any loading spring for tiredness. The last may have taken a set, preventing it being clamped up as it should and, if so, is best replaced. If a spare is not available, it may be feasible to add a spacer to achieve the desired effect, but check that this will not inhibit the correct operation of all parts. As well as the basic setting of the control knob, some friction dampers may be designed to tighten up as the forks move from their static position. This may be achieved by ramps formed by the fork parts, and these must be checked for wear and smooth operation.

Lever-arm dampers

These are much as the girder fork type, except that the disc assembly sits between two lever arms, with one end of each of these bolted to the frame and the moving part of the suspension. They require the same attention as the

Modern Girling gas shock rear unit with remote reservoir

girder fork type, plus a look at their attachments and pivot points. The lever-arm damper can be used in most applications as long as there is room for it to function fully at extreme suspension movements. It has been used on girder forks for racing and was quite common on Italian racers for a while, where it went with rear pivoted forks. In at least one of these applications, it could be adjusted by the rider, using a remote control, and was in general use in the period around World War 2.

Moto Guzzi post-war Superalce with spring units under engine and friction lever-arm dampers above rear fork

Suspension units

For most riders, this term refers to the telescopic coil spring assembly, with or without hydraulic damping, which is used to control the pivoted-fork form of rear suspension. The same items, with a change of spring, can also be found on leading-link forks and, for some of these, as a damper unit only. They may also be used to control a sidecar wheel.

Most suspension units with hydraulic damping do not lend themselves to restoration work, as the damper strut is a sealed unit. Some can be dismantled, but most cannot without cutting and machining. What can be done is to remove the spring and its covers, if any, for which you may need a compression tool. Typically, the spring sits on a collar incorporating the cam ring for preload adjustment, and is held at the top by a split collar, or a ring, with a slot through its side. To remove either means compressing the spring, which is difficult on a lightweight and just about impossible on anything larger. Make sure the tool fits correctly, is used in the right manner and cannot slip. Remember that the spring is under considerable compression and can injure or cause damage if released without care.

Once the spring and covers have been removed, the damper can be inspected for wear on the piston rod, leaks or damage. Check the damping by first moving the piston in and out slowly, and then faster. The first should provide resistance you can overcome, but the

second will stop you completely if all is well. Some will only do this when the damper is extended, as they only have rebound damping, while better ones will do this in both directions, although to a differing amount.

Sealed dampers, such as the Girling, Armstrong and Woodhead-Munroe types, common on post-war British machines, may be stripped if you have the skill and resources, but those containing gas under pressure really do need specialized equipment. The work can be done, but is tricky and should not be attempted, unless you have the knowledge and tools. If you do attempt it, find an old unit to practise on before tackling anything from a machine you are restoring, and do not neglect any safety precautions.

Fortunately, there are many alternative units available that offer improved performance and can usually be dismantled for repair in the future. Most old units can be replaced in this way, but the new ones need to be checked for closed and open lengths, the end fixings and the spring rate. Some variation may be tolerated, but make sure that when the unit is fully compressed, there is still working clearance for the tyre. Allow for both tyre fling at speed and compression of the bump stop for the worst case. Above all, do make sure that the end fixings are suitable and will not come adrift. They may include replaceable rubber bushes, which should be flanked by the mounting or a large, plain washer so that the unit can

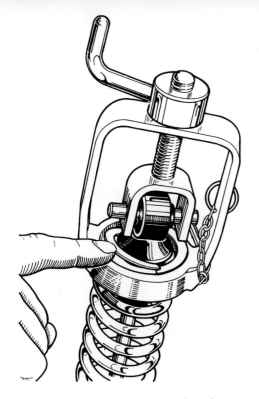

ABOVE **Tool for compressing rear unit spring so that its retaining collar and split ring can be removed**

RIGHT **AMC jampot rear unit, which can be dismantled and serviced**

attention. The damping oil should be SAE 20 viscosity and should be poured into the top filler plug until it flows from a level plug in the base. This leads to a standpipe, which sets the level and volume of oil in the unit and drains off any excess.

Francis-Barnett were one of the manufacturers of lightweight machines to make their own rear unit, but the oil in this was used as much to limit travel as to provide damping. Again, the unit can be dismantled and is a basically simple design. It is more usual to find that small machines of the early post-war period have simple spring units with no damping at all. They may well be constructed using rolled-over flanges, so cannot always be dismantled without some trouble.

For a machine in regular use, it will be well worth changing such crude units for something modern. This will provide the necessary damping and a much better ride, while keeping close to the original lines.

never detach itself from the machine, even if the bush fails.

AMC differed from many British firms in making their own rear suspension units from 1949 to 1956. These could be distinguished from others by their clevis ends, and even when the firm turned to Girling units for 1957, they kept the clevis at the lower end. It was 1963 before they fitted stock units and, thus, the rear fork details reflect this.

There were two types of AMC rear unit, the early, slim ones being referred to as 'candlesticks' and the fatter, later ones as 'jampots'. Both can be serviced, and the owners' club can help with information, tools and spares. Both types are sensitive to the volume of oil in them, but this is especially true for the candlestick version. In both cases, the procedure for filling and expelling air must be carried out exactly by the book and carefully. Capacities are 50 cc and 85 cc respectively, and both use SAE 20 oil.

Royal Enfield were another to make their own hydraulically-damped rear suspension units, using them on their Bullet and Twin models up to late 1953. They were fairly simple in their construction and can be dismantled for

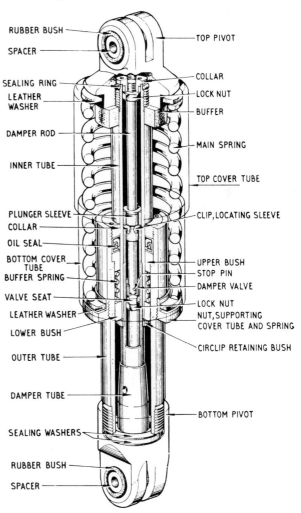

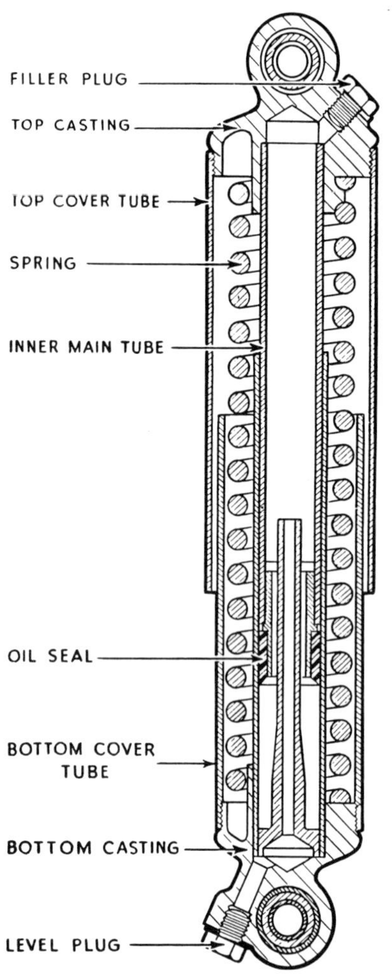
FILLER PLUG
TOP CASTING
TOP COVER TUBE
SPRING
INNER MAIN TUBE
OIL SEAL
BOTTOM COVER TUBE
BOTTOM CASTING
LEVEL PLUG

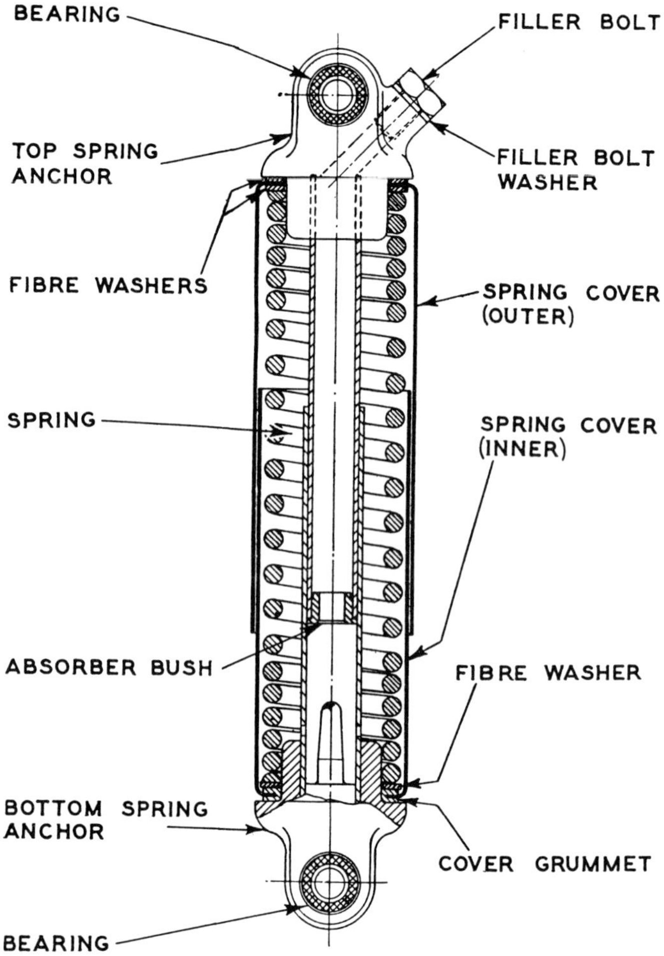
BEARING
FILLER BOLT
TOP SPRING ANCHOR
FILLER BOLT WASHER
FIBRE WASHERS
SPRING COVER (OUTER)
SPRING
SPRING COVER (INNER)
ABSORBER BUSH
FIBRE WASHER
BOTTOM SPRING ANCHOR
COVER GRUMMET
BEARING

ABOVE **Francis-Barnett rear suspension unit, which can be dismantled**

ABOVE LEFT **Rear suspension unit made and fitted by Royal Enfield on their early post-war Bullet and 500 Twin models**

Not all machines combined the suspension medium with the hydraulic damper, and examples as diverse as the Greeves scrambler and the Lambretta scooter make this point. The Vincent-HRD was similar, and that firm made its own hydraulic dampers for their C models, which had Girdraulic front forks. They fitted the damper between the two spring boxes at the rear, but retained the friction damper incorporated in the seat stays of the earlier B models.

Level-height units

A racing machine can be set up to a desired ride height by varying the length and strength of its suspension units to suit the prevailing conditions, but this is less easy with a road model. The latter has to cope with a variation between a light rider travelling alone and a heavy rider plus passenger and luggage. This can double the load on the rear suspension, and few firms offer more than the usual spring preload adjustment to compensate.

Where only the preload variation exists this can be used, but it is important that both units are set to the same position. Having one soft and one hard will not do anything for comfort, handling or the good health of the system's parts.

Air, or air-assisted suspension, offers the possibility of varying the spring rate to restore the ride height when extra loads are placed on it. The rear units and front forks are usually linked as two pairs, which makes it easier to pressurize them, and this link can be extended to a common valve and a gauge added to that.

Such a system would normally be pumped

Vincent rear suspension friction damper built into dualseat support and attached to rear fork member

up by hand, using a small plunger air pump carried in the pocket or on the machine. From this was developed a system with an electric air pump, plus control valves, so that the ride could be varied while on the move. This does involve a number of small air pipes running about the machine, plus valves and extra wiring, which adds to the complication and can introduce its own set of faults. Use the maker's instructions to deal with these, although most are likely to be basic electric or pneumatic connection problems. Make sure all air pipes are free of kinks and tight spots that could prevent the flow of air.

The final step along this road is the self-levelling rear unit produced by Boge and used by BMW under the Nivomat name. This is completely self-contained and utilizes the suspension movement to operate an internal pump that lifts the machine to its ride height. It is a clever and complex assembly that cannot be renovated without very special equipment. Do not even think of tackling one at home.

Safety note

A number of modern, and some older, suspension units contain a gas at high pressure, and these must not be tampered with. In some cases, the workshop manual will give a procedure for releasing the pressure, and if you attempt this, make sure you follow the instructions exactly and fulfil all safety requirements. If in any doubt at all, do not attempt this task and do not tamper with, or load, the unit in any way, which could cause the pressure to be released. Do not heat the units up either as this will raise the internal pressure and they could explode.

CHAPTER 8
Attachments and alignments

This chapter is concerned with the supports for the parts, which are attached to the frame. These range from the complete engine unit down to minor brackets for details. Along with engine mountings, there are torque stays, and included with this subject is the Norton Isolastic system.

Wheel alignment is the final stage of all the checks for distortion, and this leads on to changes of wheel or tyre. Engine changes also need to be considered for their effects on the frame and other cycle parts.

The sidecar is a major attachment for a motorcycle and introduces its own set of problems and needs. One is the actual technique of driving the combination, which is not dealt with here, but others include the attachment fittings, effect on fork trail, outfit alignment and increased loads on the frame, forks and wheels.

Lugs and brackets

These should have been dealt with while the frame was being attended to, and the aim is for all to be in good order and correctly aligned. Where this is not the case, it is usually necessary to heat up the part to straighten it, which is why all this work should be done before any finishing is undertaken.

The attachments invariably have one or more holes in them for bolts, and these may need some attention if damaged or distorted. They may require welding up and redrilling in the worst cases, or simply improving with a file. Where the holes are threaded, they must

be checked for the thread condition and cleaned out. Often, there will be debris at the bottom of any blind hole, and this must be removed to ensure that the fixing associated with it can be tightened fully without bottoming before it clamps.

Lugs include those built into the frame for sidecar attachment, which are commonly found on older, larger machines with brazed lug-and-tube frames. They are much less common on modern frames, and some firms even prohibit the attachment of a sidecar, although this does not always stop an enthusiastic owner.

Sidecar lugs are often threaded for an attachment, and these, too, need to be clean and free from damage if the connection is to fit as it should. The sidecar places considerable loads on its connections to the frame, so all these points must be really sound if you contemplate hitching on a chair.

Engine mountings

These are the most important of the various frame lugs and brackets, for they carry the greatest loads. They may also be part of the frame structure, where this is of the diamond type, and their condition has a bearing on strength, rigidity and machine vibration. In the past, engine mountings were invariably solid, but in more recent machines, and in earlier exceptions, may be flexible with bonded rubbers in one form or another.

Solid mountings can be connected directly to the frame or via plates, or by a combination

of both. All holes must be in good condition in frame, plate and engine, while the fixing bolts or studs must also be in order. In production machines the bolts are seldom an accurate fit in their holes, some of which may be slotted to cope with tolerances. Often, there will be one locating hole that provides a good fit, while the others will be left oversize to deal with most eventualities. Large and thick washers help the bolt or stud to clamp in place without deforming the holes or slots. They may be essential, for without them the bolt head or nut may pull into the plate material and, thus, slacken off, with potentially disastrous results.

Some machines, especially those with hand-built, special frames, will be made to a much better standard, all holes having only a working clearance on the bolt or stud passing through them. The best will have reamed holes, from which any fixing can be pulled without disturbing the others, but such standards are usually reserved for racing machines. Where employed, they will stiffen the whole structure

ABOVE **BMW R67 with sidecar to make a nice sporting outfit, but without the leading-link forks it deserves**

BELOW **Sidecar lug on downtube of BSA Golden Flash, allowing connection to chair on either side, via swan-neck tube in most cases**

and are a good standard to aim for on any machine.

Flexible mountings exist in two distinct forms. One is similar to, but lighter than, a car engine mount and allows the engine freedom in a controlled manner. The post-war Sunbeam twin models used this type, along with rubber snubbers, and the parts must be in good order and correctly adjusted if they are to function as designed.

The other type is the bonded rubber bush, which is pressed into the crankcase mountings to absorb the high-frequency vibration. With this design, the engine is constrained from side movements of any magnitude, so its rear chain drive alignment is not adversely affected. Replacement is the usual remedy if the mounting is not in good condition, but also check for any spacers that may be needed to allow it to work properly.

Ancillary to the engine mountings is the torque stay, which links the cylinder head to the frame. These come in a great variety of sizes, shapes, materials and degrees of rigidity, but all must be firmly fastened in place if they are to do their job. Some are adjustable, and all should have fixings that are a good fit.

Where there is slackness, it is best to arrange for this to be taken up so that the engine torque is reacting against solid parts. This minor step can often alter the degree of vibration felt by the rider through the seat, bars or tank, and is one possible remedy if this is a problem. Another is to slacken the engine from its fixings, jack the engine up to lift its weight, and

ABOVE **Rear engine plates on an early Royal Enfield to hold engine, link to frame lugs and support gearbox**

ABOVE LEFT **Triumph twin front engine plates surround dynamo**

BELOW **Flexible engine mountings and snubbers, as used by the post-war Sunbeam in-line twin**

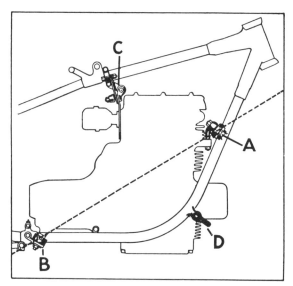

then to tighten the fixings. Again, this can alter the effects of vibration on the machine and rider.

Norton Isolastic

All Norton Commando models have this unusual system where the engine, gearbox and rear pivoted fork, complete with wheel, are isolated from the main frame. This is done with main mountings at the front and rear of the engine and gearbox assembly, plus a steady bolted to the top of the integral rocker box. Because the engine can move relative to the frame, the silencers are rubber-mounted to avoid damage to them, the exhaust pipes or their fixings.

Each main mounting is housed in a tube, the front one being welded to two plates that are bolted to the front of the crankcase. At the rear, the housing is incorporated in the rear engine plates, which are bolted to the back of the crankcase, support the gearbox and carry the pivot spindle for the rear fork.

The housing tubes are designed so that their centres coincide with fixing holes in the main frame, and between the stud or bolt in these and the tube are the isolating rubbers. At the front there are two of these, plus two smaller ones, which act as bump stops, while at the rear there are three main and two bump rubbers, except on early models, which only have two main rubbers, as at the front.

The rubbers allow the engine-to-rear-wheel assembly to move relative to the frame without

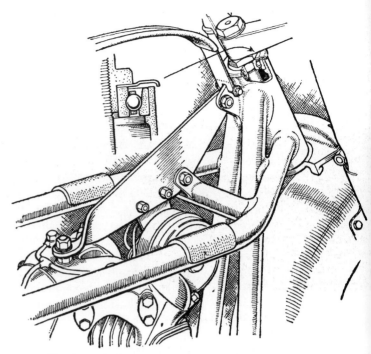

ABOVE **Head steady for Norton 88 twin in Featherbed frame**

BELOW **Section through the front and rear Isolastic mountings for the Norton Commando**

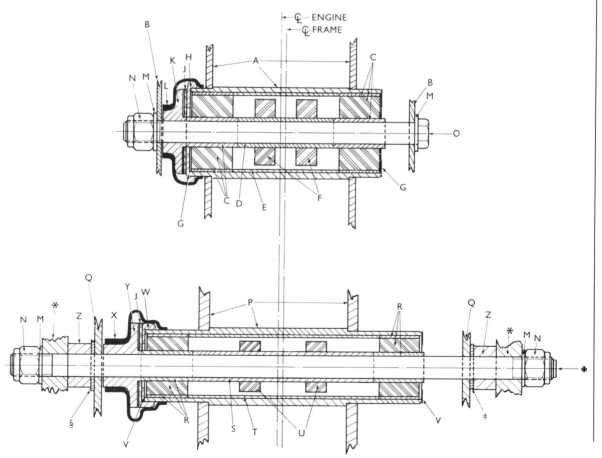

113

affecting chain alignment, while absorbing vibration. As the parts can move sideways, as well as fore and aft, this aspect has to be limited to keep the wheels in line, and this is done with collars on either side of the outer tubes. By adjusting the gap between them to a restricted amount, the desired result can be achieved, and by varying it, the handling can be tuned.

It is imperative that there is some play between the parts, as if reduced to nil, the machine will have a rigid engine mounting, for which the frame was never designed, and it will break. The gap is given as 0.010 in. by Norton, but many riders prefer to reduce this to 0.005 in. for road work, while 0.002 in. is used when racing. The smaller gap improves handling, but reduces the vibration suppression.

The gap is set by the use of shims on the early models, and a threaded adjuster for the Mk III. In either case, there are thrust washers and gaiters to impede the work, but it must be carried out precisely if the best results are sought. Shimming is easier to carry out off the machine, and the front mounting assembly is easy to remove. The rear one requires far more dismantling, but this can well repay the effort called for, and on a general restoration much of the work will occur anyway.

The rubber mounts can be renewed, as can the thrust washers, which are best replaced by the PTFE type with a bronzed look. The tube housing will need to be cleaned before assembly, while the protective gaiters must be in a good order. Grease will be needed on assembly, and the rubber or silicone type is preferred by many to ensure that the rubbers do not swell. Early machines can benefit from the addition of spacers to locate the rubbers in the tube, and the owners' club suggests that garden hose or a turn or two of tape will be quite adequate.

Wheel alignment

The final object of much of the work on the frame and forks is to ensure that the front and rear wheels are in line with each other. This is governed by other factors, as well as the frame, and these include the way in which the wheels are built on to their hubs, the disposition and size of wheel spacers, and the manner in which the rear chain tension is set.

If all the parts are as they should be, the owner will only need to deal with the last, but while doing this, it should be remembered that the rear chain sprockets need to be in line as well as the wheels. If the wheels are correctly positioned, but not the chain run, there will be rapid wear on the transmission parts, so this error will need to be corrected. Often, this can be achieved by moving the wheel over, as long as the physical constraints allow this.

Thus, all these points need to be dealt with before the wheels are aligned, and when restoring a basket job you may have to start from scratch. In such cases, you will need, but may not have, the wheel offset dimension, which

The basis of wheel alignment, which can be from the rims or the tyres, but must have all four points in a line

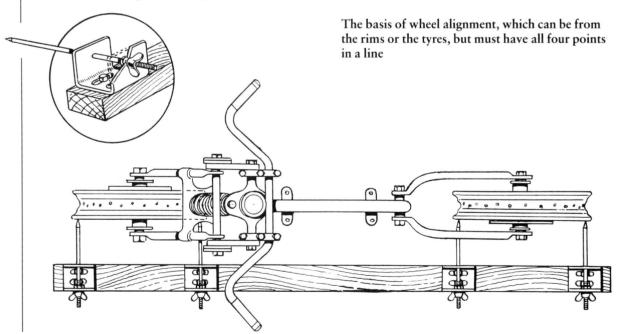

sets the rim centre relative to the hub, the rear chain offset from the centre line of the machine, and the relation of this to the wheels.

Any wheel offset figure found must be related to a rim size, as it will usually be a measurement from the edge of the brake drum to the side of the rim. Therefore, a change in size for the latter will affect the dimension. The chain offset must be sufficient to clear the rear tyre, as well as any surrounding structure and, again, any change in tyre section may be restricted by this.

If all is well, the wheels will sit on the centre line of the machine with the front one in the centre of the forks. When aligned with the rear, the chain should run smoothly between the sprockets and clear of the tyre. Any necessary adjustments may be made with spacers or by building the wheel with the rim moved over as required.

With all this in order, the wheels themselves will need to be checked for any distortion of the rim as it revolves. Any excess needs to be removed for good handling and must be done before the alignment check, as this is based on either the rim or the tyre side.

Once the tyre is seen to turn without side movement, the alignment can be checked with a straight edge. This is done along the tyre sides front and rear, as high up as possible, although the machine's parts can restrict this. Allowance must be made for any difference in tyre or rim width, and spacers of half this amount will be needed to compensate.

The straight edge can be a plank or a piece of string. The former must be really true along one edge and may need to be cut away in places to clear the machine. Its straightness can be checked with a steel edge or string, and a spacer added, if required, to allow for a tyre width difference.

The edge should be placed against both front and rear wheels and must touch each in two places. It may be necessary to set the front wheel with care to achieve this, and as this is done, the edge will move slighly at the rear. Any error should be taken out with the rear chain adjusters until the edge just touches at the four points, at which stage the wheels will be in line.

The same result can be achieved with string, which should be tied to a front wheel spoke, led round the front of the tyre and then back to the rear one. A delicate touch will be needed

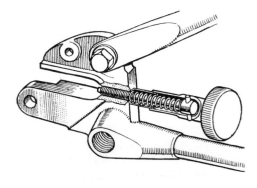

ABOVE **Chain adjuster, as fitted by Vincent and a touch better class than usual**

BELOW **Eccentric chain tension adjuster on 1971 BSA unit single, with pin holes to hold pivot in correct position**

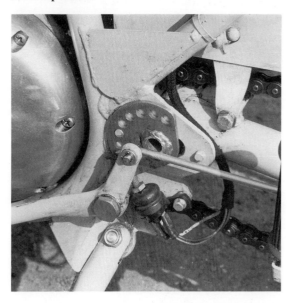

for an exact setting, but is not too hard to achieve. Make quite sure the string is clear of all other parts of the machine.

Once wheels have been aligned, it is often feasible to mark the adjusters so that they remain true to each other. A punch mark on a bolt head will suffice. The chain can then be reset and the wheels kept in line by moving each adjuster by the same amount. It can still be worth checking occasionally, especially if any frame, fork or wheel bearing is changed.

Changes

Some frames, such as the featherbed Norton, lend themselves to this and have been fitted

with all manner of different engines over the years. The Greeves is another that seems able to accommodate freely a good range of alternatives, while the BSA Bantam offers easy interchangeability, but only between the various D-series engine units.

In general, it should not be too difficult to change an engine for one of similar size and power where a cradle frame is involved. New engine plates will be needed, but these will normally pick up on the existing mountings, so the major task is quite easy. Problems are more likely to arise in dealing with the details of primary drive, rear chain line, exhaust pipes, oil lines, electrics and controls.

The Triton is possibly the best known of the engine-change specials, but there are many more. All produce the same problems, but solutions vary greatly in their degree of difficulty. In all cases, the work must be carried out following sound engineering practice, and you should not attempt anything like this, unless you are confident of your abilities to design, make and assemble the parts in a capable manner.

The same applies to fork changes, for which you must check the basic steering geometry, and wheel alterations. The last are usually less of a problem, although no less important with regard to safety and sound work, as minor alterations with spacers and spindles may be all that is needed. Do make sure that the brake anchor is strong enough to do its job and well engineered.

The sidecar

The sidecar developed from early exercises with trailers and forecars as a means of carrying a passenger and luggage on a motorcycle. It did this without incurring the cost or complexity of a car, and with the asset that the outfit could quickly revert to solo travel when desired.

The sidecar soon reached a standard form, which it kept for many years. This was based on a rigid chassis, which was attached to the motorcycle at three or four points, with a wheel mounted rigidly to it. On this chassis went a body mounted on some form of springs to give the occupant a comfortable ride.

Sidecar wheel suspension was not adopted

LEFT **Nice combination of Ariel Square Four engine and Norton Featherbed frame and other cycle parts**

ABOVE **Sidecar connection clamp used where no frame lug is provided and which must be tight**

until well into the post-war period, when machines in general had gained rear suspension. As this became more usual, the sidecar design developed with new chassis forms and monocoque construction. The body and its material also varied over the years, from wicker work in Edwardian days to steel or aluminium on wood frames, and later to all-metal or fibreglass.

A few outfits, built mainly for military use, had the sidecar wheel driven as well as the rear one, which introduced complications in the transmission rather than the frame. The wheels could still be sprung, and most such machines had forward and reverse gearboxes, plus a differential lock between the driven wheels for adverse conditions.

Sidecar effects

When a sidecar is added to a solo motorcycle, it introduces a whole set of problems of its own. The way in which the machine must be ridden differs a great deal and calls for changes in the fork geometry as well as to the suspension settings and gearing. The loads on the wheels will be increased, as will those on the frame, while the alignment and setting up is all-important to the outfits' behaviour on the road.

The attachment of the chassis to the frame is often carried out with universal fittings that will accommodate most makes and models. They attach to lugs incorporated into the frame, or bolt or clamp to it, in such a way as to spread the loads. Most work well enough, although the universal nature of the fittings can reduce their rigidity to some degree. In some cases, the fittings will be quickly detachable, and these may be of the ball-and-claw type, which allow the chair to be refitted without any need to check its alignment.

All fittings must be checked over, along with the main chassis for any signs of damage or trouble. Most problems can be overcome without much trouble, although heat and persuasion may be necessary in some cases. A number of the techniques used for tube-and-lug frames can be employed on many older chassis, while modern ones are more likely to call for the welding torch.

The addition of a sidecar will invariably mean that the machine's gearing must be

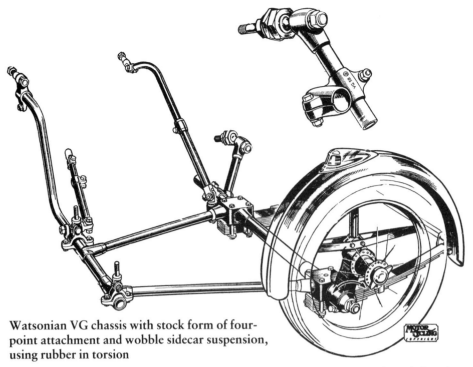

Watsonian VG chassis with stock form of four-point attachment and wobble sidecar suspension, using rubber in torsion

lowered, which is easy with chain drive, but not so with a shaft. The reduction may vary from 10 to 25 per cent and depends on the power characteristics of the engine and the type of sidecar to be added. With chain drive, the alteration may be made at any, or all, sprockets, depending on whether there is unit construction, but normally it is carried out at the engine sprocket where this restriction does not apply.

The sidecar calls for much less trail than a solo, and this can easily be adjusted on girder forks by changing one of the pairs of fork links. It is more of a problem with telescopics, and few offer any alternative, so their steering becomes heavy. Some allow for adjustment or alternative parts, but as the telescopic fork is so weak in withstanding side loads, it is common practice on modern outfits to replace it with long leading-links. These offer far more rigidity, ease of trail adjustment and a ready choice of suspension units.

A steering damper is used much more on a sidecar outfit than a solo and, if not fitted as standard, should be added. It must be able to cope with the full fork movement from lock to lock, which may be more than that of a solo to give a good turning circle. The forks, and the suspension at the rear, will probably need to be stiffer than for a solo in order to cope with the extra weight of the sidecar. Stronger

springs were listed for this purpose by many firms, while rear units have their own, which can easily be changed.

The wheels may need attention, as they will be subject to much higher loads. This can call for heavier-gauge spokes, especially for the rear wheel. Bearings, too, can suffer, so may need changing more often. The tyres should be more suited to sidecar work, but will then wear to be unusable in solo form, and any change could affect the speedometer drive gearing. This last will be altered if the drive is from the gearbox and the gearing changed at the box or rear wheel sprockets, but most models of that type have alternative drive gears for the box to suit the situation.

The brakes may need uprating, while the addition of a sidecar wheel brake will call for some means of operating it. This can be by a separate pedal beside the rear one, through a link with the rear, or by hydraulic operation with one pedal working shoes or pads at all three wheels. This last is not easy to set up due to the differing loads needed by each brake.

Finally, there are the electrics to attend to, with extra front and rear lights to comply with your local legislation. Some owners use the additional space of the sidecar to fit an extra-large battery, which can be useful in some circumstances.

LEFT **Harley-Davidson sidecar outfit with most of the trimmings**

BELOW **Canterbury sidecar chassis with trailing-arm wheel suspension controlled by stock Girling unit**

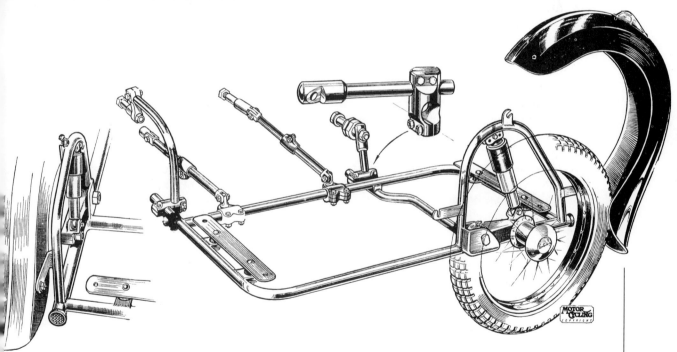

Sidecar suspension

For many years, the sidecar wheel was rigidly attached to the chassis, as most owners distrusted suspension for it or the machine rear wheel. Even in the post-war years, this attitude persisted for some time, with some firms continuing to offer rigid or plunger frames essentially for their sidecar customers only.

In time, this did change, and from the 1950s outfits increasingly appeared with sidecar wheel suspension. It took a variety of forms, some as much as on the motorcycle itself, the wheel being on a trailing arm or a vertical one and able to wobble to and fro. The suspension medium was as varied as on the motorcycle, with conventional spring-and-damper units,

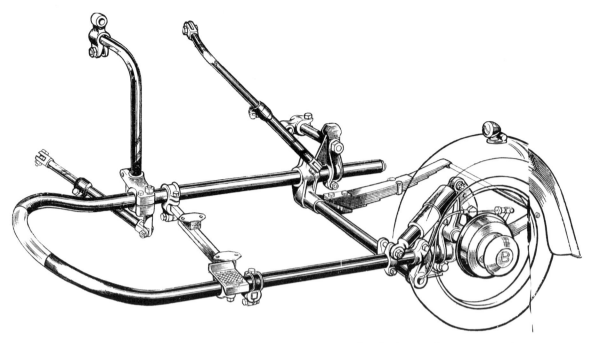

Blacknell sidecar chassis with trailing-arm wheel suspension incorporating bell-crank link to Armstrong unit

tension springs, or rubber in shear or torsion all being used.

Repair and renovation of the suspension system should be carried out in the same manner as for the main frame, and involves the arm holding the wheel, its bearing and its support. Cleaning, checking and mending follow the same lines as other similar parts, while safety and the loads carried by the details must always be borne in mind.

Assembly should be easy, but with the same strictures on safety and special care regarding wheel and suspension clearance. This must allow for the full wheel movement, together with that of any associated parts, while not omitting to cater for movement of the sidecar body on its own springs. These may be designed to restrict the travel in some planes, but there must be clearance to cover all circumstances to avoid a clash of parts.

Sidecar alignment

This makes all the difference between an outfit being hard work to drive or light and easy. It requires the setting of toe-in, lean-out and wheel lead, plus the mounting of the body to the chassis, and some of it is subjective. To a degree, the settings depend on the type of side-

car involved, the performance and suspension of the motorcycle, and your driving style.

The alignment should be checked and adjusted on a flat, level floor and will require two straight edges, a plumb line and measuring equipment. Begin by checking the general alignment of the chassis to the floor and its height at front and rear. It should be parallel for the first and nose up by about $1\frac{1}{2}$ in. for the second.

The toe-in is the next setting to check, and this is the amount by which the sidecar wheel points in to the machine at the front. To check it, place a straight plank against the machine's tyres with any packing needed to compensate for tyre width variation. This will give a line along the machine, and a similar one will be needed along the sidecar wheel, for which a second plank will be required. The distance between them should be measured just ahead of the front wheel and aft of the rear. The front should be shorter than the rear, the difference being the toe-in, which is usually $\frac{1}{2}$–$\frac{3}{4}$ in.

Next is the lean-out, which is the amount by which the machine leans away from the sidecar. It is measured at the top of the forks using a plumb line hung from the handlebars. Dimensions from this to the centre of the bars at the top and centre of the tyre at ground level give the lean-out, which is normally $\frac{1}{2}$–1 in. These two settings govern the way in which the outfit will run on a straight, cambered road and how it will drive round corners. If well set up,

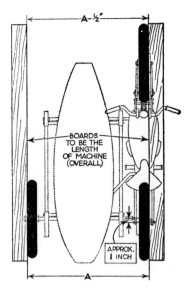

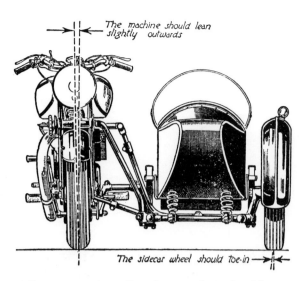

Sidecar alignment features of toe-in and wheel lead, which partly govern the way the outfit behaves on the road

The motorcycle needs to lean out from the sidecar to combat the effects of the road camber

it will result in pleasant and easy handling.

The third dimension involved in setting up varies a good deal more and is the lead the sidecar wheel has over the rear one. It may be as low as 1 in. on a pre-war side-valve model with girder forks that is pulling a heavy touring chair. At the other end of the scale, with a sports outfit, the lead may be as much as 9 in. The exact figure will affect the outfit's behaviour when cornering, and the owner must strike a balance to suit the outfit and driving style. For a start, a figure of 4–6 in. should give an acceptable result.

Before checking the outfit on the road, go round all the fixings and make sure every one is done up tight. Once tried, you may wish to experiment a little with the settings, which is worth doing, as it will give you a feel for how alterations affect the handling. From this should come your own set of optimum dimensions.

The actual driving of an outfit is another problem to solve, which will give you great enjoyment when you have cracked it. On the way there, it can generate some surprises, so practice with some caution.

Appendices

1 Threads, spanners and inserts

The tables below show thread type, diameter, threads per inch (or pitch), spanner size, and tapping drill size for the thread itself and for a HeliCoil wire thread insert. These last two are given in millimetres or inches. The latter may refer to a size in the letter and number series of drills, so engineering tables should be consulted on this.

Thread form	Dia.	tpi	A/F spanner	Tapping drill size Thread	HeliCoil
BSF	$\frac{1}{4}$	26	.445 in.	$\frac{13}{64}$ in.	6.6 mm
55 degrees	$\frac{5}{16}$	22	.525 in.	.257 in.	8.3 mm
	$\frac{3}{8}$	20	.600 in.	8.0 mm	9.8 mm
	$\frac{7}{16}$	18	.710 in.	9.4 mm	$\frac{29}{64}$ in.
	$\frac{1}{2}$	16	.820 in.	10.8 mm	$\frac{33}{64}$ in.
	$\frac{9}{16}$	16	.920 in.	12.4 mm	$\frac{37}{64}$ in.
Whitworth	$\frac{1}{8}$	40	.338 in.	2.4 mm	3.3 mm
55 degrees	$\frac{3}{16}$	24	.445 in.	.136 in.	5.0 mm
	$\frac{1}{4}$	20	.525 in.	.189 in.	6.7 mm
	$\frac{5}{16}$	18	.600 in.	.246 in.	$\frac{21}{64}$ in.
	$\frac{3}{8}$	16	.710 in.	7.6 mm	$\frac{25}{64}$ in.
	$\frac{7}{16}$	14	.820 in.	8.9 mm	$\frac{29}{64}$ in.
	$\frac{1}{2}$	12	.920 in.	10.1 mm	$\frac{33}{64}$ in.
	$\frac{9}{16}$	12	1.010 in.	11.7 mm	$\frac{37}{64}$ in.
Cycle	$\frac{1}{8}$	40		.098 in.	
60 degrees	$\frac{5}{32}$	32		.123 in.	
	$\frac{3}{16}$	32		.154 in.	
	$\frac{7}{32}$	26	.413 in.	.178 in.	
	$\frac{1}{4}$	26	.445 in.	.209 in.	
	$\frac{9}{32}$	26		.240 in.	
	$\frac{5}{16}$	26	.525 in.	.271 in.	

APPENDICES

Thread form	Dia.	tpi	A/F spanner	Tapping drill size Thread	HeliCoil
	$\frac{3}{8}$	26	.600 in.	.334 in.	
	$\frac{7}{16}$	26	.710 in.	.396 in.	
	$\frac{1}{2}$	26	.820 in.	.459 in.	
	$\frac{9}{16}$	26	.920 in.	.521 in.	
	$\frac{5}{8}$	26	1.010 in.	.584 in.	
	$\frac{11}{16}$	26	1.100 in.	.646 in.	
	$\frac{3}{4}$	26	1.200 in.	.709 in.	
	$\frac{7}{16}$	20	.710 in.	.384 in.	
	$\frac{1}{2}$	20	.820 in.	.447 in.	
	$\frac{9}{16}$	20	.920 in.	.509 in.	
	$\frac{5}{8}$	20	1.010 in.	.572 in.	
	$\frac{11}{16}$	20	1.100 in.	.634 in.	
	$\frac{3}{4}$	20	1.200 in.	.697 in.	
BSP 55 degrees	$\frac{1}{8}$	28		.339 in.	$\frac{25}{64}$ in.
	$\frac{1}{4}$	19		$\frac{29}{64}$ in.	$\frac{17}{32}$ in.
	$\frac{3}{8}$	19		$\frac{19}{32}$ in.	$\frac{43}{64}$ in.
	$\frac{1}{2}$	14		.739 in.	$\frac{27}{32}$ in.
UNF 60 degrees	$\frac{1}{4}$	28	.437 in.	.213 in.	6.6 mm
	$\frac{5}{16}$	24	.500 in.	.228 in.	8.2 mm
	$\frac{3}{8}$	24	.562 in.	.332 in.	9.8 mm
	$\frac{7}{16}$	20	.625 in.	$\frac{25}{64}$ in.	$\frac{29}{64}$ in.
	$\frac{1}{2}$	20	.750 in.	$\frac{29}{64}$ in.	$\frac{33}{64}$ in.
	$\frac{9}{16}$	18	.812 in.	$\frac{33}{64}$ in.	$\frac{37}{64}$ in.
UNC 60 degrees	$\frac{1}{4}$	20	.437 in.	.201 in.	6.7 mm
	$\frac{5}{16}$	18	.500 in.	.257 in.	$\frac{21}{64}$ in.
	$\frac{3}{8}$	16	.562 in.	.312 in.	$\frac{25}{64}$ in.
	$\frac{7}{16}$	14	.625 in.	.368 in.	$\frac{29}{64}$ in.
	$\frac{1}{2}$	13	.750 in.	$\frac{27}{64}$ in.	$\frac{33}{64}$ in.
	$\frac{9}{16}$	12	.812 in.	$\frac{31}{64}$ in.	14.75 mm
BA 47½ degrees	0	1.00 mm	.413 in.	.191 in	6.2 mm
	1	0.90 mm	.365 in.	4.3 mm	5.5 mm
	2	0.81 mm	.324 in.	.1495 in.	4.9 mm
	3	0.73 mm	.282 in.	.1285 in.	4.3 mm
	4	0.66 mm	.248 in.	2.85 mm	3.8 mm
	5	0.59 mm	.220 in.	.0995 in.	3.3 mm
	6	0.53 mm	.193 in.	2.2 mm	2.9 mm
Metric	6	1.0	10 mm	4.6 mm	6.2 mm
	7	1.0	11 mm	5.6 mm	7.2 mm

Thread form	Dia.	Pitch	A/F spanner	Tapping drill size	
				Thread	HeliCoil
	8	1.0	13 mm		8.2 mm
	8	1.25	13 mm	6.3 mm	8.3 mm
	9	1.25	16 mm	7.3 mm	9.3 mm
	10	1.25	17 mm		10.3 mm
	10	1.5	17 mm	7.95 mm	10.3 mm
	11	1.5		8.95 mm	11.3 mm
	12	1.25	19 mm		12.3 mm
	12	1.75	19 mm	9.7 mm	12.4 mm
	14	1.5	22 mm		14.3 mm
	14	2.0	22 mm	11.3 mm	14.4 mm

Odd cycle threads that may be found on older machines

Thread form	Dia.	tpi	Tapping drill size	Notes
Cycle	$\frac{17}{64}$	26	.225 in.	
	$\frac{7}{8}$	24	.831 in.	
	$\frac{31}{32}$	30	.933 in.	
	1	24	.956 in.	
	$1\frac{1}{8}$	26	1.084 in.	
	1.29	24	1.246 in.	Left-hand
	1.37	24	1.326 in.	Left- and right-hand
	1.45	26	1.409 in.	Left- and right-hand
	$1\frac{9}{16}$	24	1.518 in.	Left-hand
	$1\frac{5}{8}$	24	1.581 in.	

2 Loctite

There is a range of chemical products used mainly for locking and retaining under the Loctite name. Used in the right manner, they can be very useful and will overcome many problems. Most troubles occur because parts have not been cleaned, but also remember that Loctite may have a shelf life, especially once opened. Normally, this is at least 12 months, so it should not be too much of a problem. However, it does mean that any with an unknown history should be treated with care, unless you are certain of both the grade and the age of what has come to hand.

The list below is a small selection from the full range, but should include those needed for frame and fork work.

222 Screwlock. Low-strength thread lock for small screws. Gap fills 0.006 in. on diameter.

242 Nutlock or Lock'N'Seal. Medium-strength thread lock for nuts and bolts. Gap fills 0.006 in. on diameter.

262 Threadlocker. Extra high strength for heavy shock, vibration or stress levels. Similar to 270.

270 Studlock. High-strength thread lock for parts not normally dismantled. Gap fills 0.01 in. on diameter.

271 Stud'N'Bearing Fit. As 270. Also used for bearings and similar round items. See also 641.

601 Retainer. High-strength retention of parts on to shafts. Gap fills 0.004 in. on diameter.

638 Retainer High Strength. Stronger version of 601. Gap fills 0.006 in. on diameter.

641 Bearing Fit. Used on bearings in housings to overcome creep. Gap fills 0.006 in. on diameter.

660 Quick Metal. Used on worn shafts to improve fit with static parts. Gap fills 0.02 in. Useful on splines and keyways, or as an extra-strong thread lock.

Index